# Letters to the Church

# Letters to the Church

### Encouragement and Engagement
### for the 2020 Election

## William B. Kincaid

WIPF & STOCK · Eugene, Oregon

LETTERS TO THE CHURCH
Encouragement and Engagement for the 2020 Election

Wipf & Stock
An Imprint of Wipf and Stock Publishers
199 W. 8th Ave., Suite 3
Eugene, OR 97401

www.wipfandstock.com

PAPERBACK ISBN: 978-1-7252-6710-7
HARDCOVER ISBN: 978-1-7252-6711-4
EBOOK ISBN: 978-1-7252-6712-1

Manufactured in the U.S.A.                                      05/28/20

With thanksgiving for all who are engaging
compassionately and constructively
this election season.
We need you every one.

# Contents

*Preface* | ix

*Introduction* | 1

1. A Letter to the Minister | 14
2. A Letter to the Congregation | 20

**WHAT WE ARE EXPERIENCING NOW** | 27
3. Often On Edge and Off Balance | 29
4. A Craving for Certainty | 35
5. People Reduced to a Single Dimension | 41
6. The Revival of Deadly Prejudices | 47
7. Unresolved Grief and the Tenderness Deficit | 53
8. A Desire to Be Hopeful and Helpful | 59

**WHAT WE HOPE FOR** | 67
9. To See Ourselves in the American Family Portrait | 69
10. To Know and Trust One Another Again | 76
11. To See Courageous Leadership Exercised | 82
12. To Observe and Participate in Honest Debate and Real Conversations | 89
13. For Clarity between Ethical Commitments and Political Advantage | 96
14. To Abide in an Unfailing Center in the Midst of Change | 103

**WHAT WE ARE CALLED TO** | 111

   15. To Share in Acts of Confession, Vocation, and Justice | 113

   16. To Think Carefully and Critically | 119

   17. To Prepare for Conflict | 126

   18. To Support When We Can, to Resist When We Must | 133

   19. To Find Allies When Possible | 139

   20. To Engage Constructively | 146

Now That the Election Is Over | 152

*Bibliography* | 159

# Preface

MANY VIEW THE UPCOMING presidential election as a critical one, though they do so for different reasons. Trump supporters believe the president has made a good start on his agenda and deserves more time to finish his work. Those who oppose the president cite his personal style, morality and policies as dire concerns. They also may still be stinging a bit from the 2016 election.

A democracy brings its own set of messy challenges. To highlight the role of faith and to focus on the witness of the church adds layers of complication to the messiness. This book does not call for the church to take a particular side in this or any other election, but to be the church and to bear witness to the Light in all seasons, including one in which an important election will take place.

Any credible discussion of the witness of the church involves contextualization. We cannot escape what is going on around us when we are reflecting on the life of faith and how it plays out both in the church and the culture in which we live.

Nor can we force the priorities of our faith into abstraction. Love, peace and justice are not real until they take on concrete commitments and expression. And when they fail to take on concrete expression, we must look at ourselves within the church and at the powers and principalities to find and mend the breakdown.

In other words, though I have written these letters to my sisters and brothers in the church to call us to a renewed witness in the world, it is impossible to show what needs to characterize that witness apart from shining a light on situations where we have failed to prioritize love, peace and justice in our discourse and in our policies. I have tried to be fair and informed in shining that light in these pages. I have criticized both Democrats and Republicans. I also have lifted up people from both parties as wise examples. But first and foremost, I have drawn on the depth and breadth of the Christian story so that we reaffirm our identity and values in this and every season.

I am yet to mention this project to anyone who did not respond with gratitude that I was undertaking it. We will see if the finished product is what they had in mind, but even if it isn't, I give thanks for their encouragement and for the attention they are paying to the 2020 U.S. presidential election.

As always, I am very grateful to my wife Rhonda for enthusiastically supporting this project with both her words and her understanding of the time it takes to conceive, develop and complete a project like this. I also want to thank my Christian Theological Seminary colleagues for their interest and helpful conversations, especially Dr. Dan Moseley, Dr. Frank Thomas and our Dean, Dr. Leah Gunning Francis, whose very thoughtful shepherding of my transition back to the faculty after serving as interim president allowed me to complete this time-sensitive project so that it will be available to individuals and groups prior to the November 3, 2020 election.

Most of all, I want to thank Dr. Ron Allen. I was ready to give up on this book on several occasions and would have done so had it not been for Ron's belief in this idea, his unfailingly wise feedback on several of the letters and his project-saving encouragement. Ron's distinguished career as a scholar and teacher is well known beyond the CTS community. As a senior colleague at CTS who could have focused only on his own interests and projects, Ron continued to mentor new faculty and carry a significant faculty workload of committee assignments and institutional responsibilities right up until his retirement. In doing so, he modeled for the rest of us what a good colleague looks like. He has done that again with his availability, critique and support of this book. I am deeply grateful to him and I am inspired by his example to be that kind of colleague for others.

# COVID-19

I knew that things related to the presidential election would change, perhaps even change drastically, between the time of this book's publication and Election Day. I even acknowledge that at different points in these letters. At the time, however, I thought the biggest unknowns would pertain directly to the campaign season and the election itself.

Enter COVID-19. As it turns out, things changed drastically before the book was even released. I submitted the manuscript soon after New York City officials confirmed their first cases in mid-January. I am adding this section to the book in mid-May, at which time the US case total tops 1.5 million and the death toll has eclipsed 90,000.

Fear and grief continue to grip much of the country. The economic fallout compares to the Great Depression of the 1930s. Massive uncertainty remains about the dangers of reopening businesses, schools and public places, as well as about the chances of developing effective therapies and a vaccine. The disproportionate impact of this virus on people of color and on impoverished, underserved communities has exposed again tragic disparities and systemic injustices.

Articles, posts and books already flood the conversation, all addressing various angles of this pandemic. As we continue to look toward the 2020 US presidential election, I offer three thoughts for this COVID-19 section.

First, even though I urge our collective engagement on every page here, we must stop and acknowledge how much more difficult that is going to be given our fragile state. Even before the coronavirus spread across the world, we in the United States exhibited a lot of anxiety. Many of us felt nearly constantly off-balance because of President Trump's temperament and style of governing.

The apprehension we were already feeling will continue at some level for the next several months, at least. Conflict over certain issues will escalate. Efforts to control the narrative for political and economic gain will accelerate. The push to reopen quickly and the insistence on moving cautiously will collide. Caught in the middle will be those of us who were struggling in the first place to engage. It is difficult in that condition to engage tough issues with people who hold strong, opposing views. This threatens to undermine our willingness and ability to engage topics and situations that are critical to the 2020 presidential election.

In Letter 7, I talk about God's tenderness toward Jerusalem when the city lay in ruins. God models tenderness for the Israelites so that they will incorporate that into their own life together. This is a time for us to appreciate the need for tenderness in our life together as a country. It is an opportunity to trust tenderness with ourselves and with each other. Doing so does not mean we give up on thoughtful, compassionate, justice-oriented priorities, nor does it suggest that we dial back how strongly we believe in our country's best path forward, but we also must take our fragility into consideration as we engage. Some days, we will need to step back from the action and care for ourselves. Some days, we will need to walk away from those who try to use bombast and bullying to hide their own fragility and insecurities. Tender souls also can be fierce advocates. They may be fragile themselves at times, but they know to trust tenderness when the lives of real people are at stake.

Second, our thinking toward the future of our country must match the long-term impacts of this virus. COVID-19 is far from over. More waves are on the horizon, but even after we develop effective therapies and vaccines we will continue to experience the impact of this pandemic in the way we approach our lives, think about the world, and live with each other. I know how concerned people are about the economics of this situation, but any vision for our life together that does not take into consideration the long-term spiritual, psychological and emotional effects of this virus falls short of the need.

We have learned that the Obama administration developed and left a "pandemic playbook" to the new administration. We do not know how adequate that playbook's strategies were or the extent to which the Trump administration consulted the playbook. What is clear is that the virus still caught us off-guard. We cannot ignore at first and then respond slowly to another developing storm, whether it is a virus or a climate issue or community violence or an international threat. And we cannot allow our levels of preparation, or our medical research, or our public health infrastructure to be continuously depleted.

But that is only one piece of the long-term vision. This virus has shown how negligent our partisan rancor has caused us to be. It has intensified every issue I write about in this book and created even more urgency than before for constructive resolutions. The extreme political positions and actions of a few left us vulnerable to something that is going to change our country for a long time to come. If we continue in our unwillingness to bridge differences and creatively collaborate, we will not arrive at a vision that can restore our well-being, our good place in the world and, eventually, our economy. On the other hand, if the president and other leaders will diffuse the hateful rhetoric, repudiate the misinformation, take seriously what experts in the scientific community can offer and unite the country across our many divisions, we may have a chance for a future worth pursuing. All of us can and must play a role in doing these things in the communities of which we are a part.

Third, we are reminded of where we can find our heroes. They go about their work in normal times with calm and clarity. Sometimes it takes an extraordinary time for us to notice. I lift up especially healthcare personnel and first responders. The way you risk yourselves for the sake of others inspires all of us. Some governors are showing unusual wisdom and courage day after day. Congress has approved two major pieces of relief legislation and is working on another one as I write. Bourbon distilleries are producing hand sanitizer and auto manufacturers are making ventilators. Ministers and other religious leaders are shepherding their communities through unknown territory with great care and learning, especially when it comes to staying connected by way of various technologies and platforms. Grocery store clerks, warehouse workers and truck drivers fill and deliver necessary items to homes and organizations. Musicians from little known high schools and world stages alike join in virtual ensembles to inspire us with familiar songs and moving arrangements. Add to this partial list all who have reworked and adapted their days and circumstances in order to make the best of a very bad situation.

I have told friends that I believe President Trump has the opportunity to be a hero in all of this. Some find that utterly unpalatable, as if they could not accept or appreciate any positive outcome if the president has a hand in its success. Most find the idea highly improbable. That is the group into which I fall. I do not believe I have ever witnessed someone so reluctant or incapable of being a hero as President Trump. His interest in uniting the country seems almost nonexistent, despite his inaugural pledge to be a president to all the people. Instead, to cite one example of fostering division and keeping the nation on edge, he acknowledges the authority of governors while at the same time he stokes those protesting in the state capitals. Any president would find leading in this time to be incredibly challenging, but most would attempt to set aside blatant political attacks in order to pull the country together through both empathy and economic relief, encouragement and broad governmental collaboration.

What seems more likely is that people like Governor Andy Beshear will emerge as someone we will remember very favorably from all of this. Every afternoon, Governor Beshear tells the people of Kentucky: "We'll get through this together." I think we are all eager to hear more leaders who want to bring *everybody* along in a hopeful, healthy journey into the new world that is becoming.

We went into COVID-19 a divided country. How we emerge from it will depend on how we move through this challenging time. If we continue to batter each other though this pandemic, our life beyond COVID-19 will suffer as a result. On the other hand, if we turn toward one another in mutual well-being, we will move beyond this pandemic as kinder, more appreciative and more open-minded people. If we make a promise to see each other through this season, a promise that transcends all the false lines we have drawn between one another, we will begin to reap the benefits of that spirit even now.

# Introduction

"Our country finally is going in the right direction."
    "Are you kidding? Our country is headed over a cliff!"

"Donald Trump is restoring the United States to its founding vision and original commitments."
    "No, no. Donald Trump is working frantically to reverse years of enlightened progress, equitable polices, and broad inclusion."

"The church should aggressively involve itself in the political process whenever possible and at every level."
    "What? The church should mind its own business by tending to spiritual matters and ignoring contemporary social, political, racial, ethnic, and economic issues."

## The Same Story, but Different Truths

Does any of this sound familiar? Perhaps all of it does. These extreme differences of opinion confront us almost daily through tweets, social media posts, push notifications, and unending news cycles.

Two people listen to the same speech and hear radically different messages. Two groups read the very same tweet; one group takes heart, the other one collapses in despair. As Ross Douthat puts it, "We read the same story and see different truths in it."[1]

---

1. Douthat, "Stories That Divide Us."

Douthat, of course, represents the very complexity I am describing. Some will ask, "How conservative can Douthat really be if he associates—not to mention, earns his living—with the left-wing socialists at the *New York Times*?" Others will wonder why the *New York Times* would feature a columnist who focuses so much energy on the substance and future of conservative causes.

Many of us do not see ourselves as occupying the extremes. We do not base the whole of the faith or the political process on one or two issues, but we are being pushed in that direction, even when we have no interest in going there.

Shrill extremes show up at nearly every turn. We listen to and affirm the outlets and platforms that represent what we already believe to be the case, while filtering out anything that would challenge our established positions and underlying prejudices. We embrace that which we have already embraced as true. Then, all other beliefs, opinions, and positions must be discredited, demeaned, and dismissed, lest our truth be diluted and our base of support compromised. Echo chambers on both the Left and the Right reinforce existing and highly unpragmatic policies and solutions, leaving elected bodies in gridlock and individual citizens free to act as they best see fit, even when that means reckless rhetoric, violence, and destruction.

We so seldomly talk with each other, whether it's a family member at a reunion, our neighbor next door, or a longtime international ally. At best, we lob rhetorical bombs at our opposing corners, often in not more than 280 characters. Those attacks, tragically, often land in the broad center where, until recently, constructive conversation and engagement could occur for the sake of the common good. As it is now, those in the broad center are shell-shocked, left to call into question their own commitments and loyalties. This leaves people particularly vulnerable to be clawed toward a political or religious or social extreme by those wanting to solidify their base and conquer their opponents. The idea of working with those with whom we disagree to ease suffering and realize possibilities seems to be passé. A vacuum ensues that cries out for a thoughtful, compassionate voice.

*Introduction*

We no longer have a far-reaching public discourse that calls people together to pursue the common good. Instead, we so often have two sides that move farther apart every day as a result of speech and behavior that until recently would have been regarded as embarrassing and irresponsible. While we spend days angry at the rhetoric and anxious about the dangerous fallout of the extremes, all kinds of corporate ventures fill the vacuum while we aren't looking and create a life for us from which it is nearly impossible to disentangle.

Sometimes the anxiety is so great and the dash to the extremes is so fast that we create idols and demand others bow down before those idols to prove their own loyalty, even if they are clinging to things that in any other season they would never embrace. That is the power and effect of fear and anxiety. We support candidates because we agree with them on abortion or universal healthcare or student loan forgiveness, but then have to hold our noses when we vote for them because of the temperament, morality, and rashness they exhibit on numerous other positions. When gross and obscene stories emerge about candidates, we find ourselves in a bind that, while not entirely new, feels more constricting and humiliating than in past years. It is not a good sign or a good feeling if we cringe when we cast our vote for the least offensive candidate.

Our fear and suspicion of each other, as well as our craving for certainty, cause us to retreat to our corners where positions take on zealous extremes. In the process, of course, those who hold different positions—or don't hold them fervently enough to satisfy the gatekeepers of narrow and rigid positions—are judged to be unpatriotic and faithless.

The sobering result is that we are no longer confident about what we once believed to be true and appropriate. We aren't sure we still know what we know. And we are uncertain whether we can continue to trust what we trust. We are left to question, "Is the world suddenly more chaotic and brutal than it used to be, or is this the way the world always is and we are just now discovering that?" The question stops us in our tracks and, more often than not, we as individuals and as the church, withdraw to silence, confusion, and powerlessness.

We know from Scripture that we are marvelously and wonderfully made. We know from our best moments together that our diversity enriches and elevates our shared life. And yet, we participate in the sin of defining each other in one-dimensional terms. This, of course, is not new. Those with power and privilege always have utilized this pressure, summing up other people's humanity in a single, often vulgar word or phrase in order to control and oppress another group of people. By contrast, *we* should get to decide how we want to be known. How we approach each other says something important about not just who we are, but also the kind of relationship we want to enjoy. Jesus set the example for this. "I do not call you servants, . . . I have called you friends."[2]

Unfortunately, and sometimes tragically, what continues to happen is that some very clever political strategists and elected officials use every resource at their disposal to capture us with a single dimension and, once defined, convince us we shouldn't associate, much less collaborate, with people whose singular dimension is different from our own. In other words, if I am pro-life and you are pro-choice, a great gulf exists between us that, by this new standard, rules out any notion that we can work together to reduce the number of unwanted pregnancies. And if we are at odds on the abortion issue, it's likely that difference will prevent us from working together on other issues and circumstances that hinder people's well-being and undermine the common good in our country. In some cases, people and groups are powerless to resist this imposed definition. In other cases, our silence allows us to be defined and used in this way.

The debates of our time, especially in the lead-up to and in the aftermath of the 2020 election, desperately cry out for the voices and perspectives that are marginalized and silent. When we make room for those compassionate voices and thoughtful perspectives, those who drive wedges between us and our neighbors for political gain lose their traction and influence. We can seize the

2. John 15:15.

4

opening to reclaim our voice and pursue the good and fair world that God desires for all of us, but that only happens if thoughtful, compassionate people reject the extremism, begin talking and working alongside each other, and renew the church's vocation to be light to the world.

## Regaining Our Bearings

As we approach the 2020 election, we need to regain our bearings as Christians so that we can embrace more faithfully and purposefully that calling. At present, our country remains trapped in a darkness that sets us against one another, unable to deal with our losses and unwilling to look upon each other with a shared hope and purpose.

Whether you love Donald Trump or despise him, most everyone agrees that he masterfully keeps people and the country off-balance. Sometimes those people include his closest advisors as they watch him make a public statement in the morning, then that afternoon push for a very different position in a meeting, and then return in a late evening to tweet a still different position. For example, his fluctuation on sensible gun control policies following the El Paso and Dayton mass murders in August 2019 provides one example of this. A fairly bold initial statement withered after a single call from the NRA.

We don't know very much about Mr. Trump's financial position, but he operates enough businesses and facilities around the world for us to know he's made a lot of deals in his life. No doubt, a key strategy in his dealmaking repertoire involves keeping other parties in the deal off balance. "Sorry, it's the way I negotiate," he said following the 2019 G7 Summit when asked about his many mixed messages at that gathering of world leaders.

It appears to work for him as a businessperson. Some believe it works for him as a president, too. Others do not. Wherever you stand on the question, whether you find the constant guessing about what he might say or do next and the subsequent feeling of being off-balance as commendable or deplorable, whether it is a fitting approach to governance or not, it's hard to deny that Donald Trump is a master at this approach. What remains unclear is whether this represents an "art of the deal"[3] approach to everything, or is the result of a lack of understanding and direction on critical issues and alliances. If it's the latter, he wouldn't be the first US president to stumble before the complexity of challenges and situations. Nor would he be, if it is the former, the first chief executive to deliberate shrewdly with domestic leaders and international counterparts. Our lack of confidence in knowing which it is raises anxiety and fosters fear for many on an almost daily basis.

Much to the dismay of many, the decentering that we feel did not start with Donald Trump. Nor will it end on the last day of his presidency. This time often is referred to as the era of Trump, but that's less because of the timeframe of his presidency and more the result of how he has taken advantage of the political vacuum created by massive social, economic, and population shifts around the world. It's the era of Trump in the United States, but leaders of numerous countries are capitalizing on fear and anxiety as those once faraway changes play out close to home. The losses have left many people scrambling to protect what is left of their lives and, whenever there is an opening, to try and restore all that has been lost. This often sends people to extreme positions in their search for security, safety, and their previously privileged place in their community and in the world.

But not everything that has been lost should be restored. White Supremacy is just one example. If we are going to restore something, let's restore the best version of the United States, not the worst, and finally face with honesty, humility, and determination those issues and circumstances that, as a country, we are yet to resolve equitably.

To be unsure about what we know and uncertain what to trust is a terrible way to enter an election season and a terrifying way to discern who will earn our support as election day draws near. We live in an important season as a country and we face a massively critical election in November 2020. If we are unsure about what

3. Trump, *Art of the Deal.*

is true, if we are uncertain about what values should shape our future as individuals and a country, how can we know who the best candidate is in a given race?

## The Witness of the Church

What difference will your faith make in the way you think about and participate in the 2020 presidential election? I wrote this book with the hope of prompting honest conversations, sparking a renewal of courageous imagination, and spurring Christians in the United States toward constructive engagement in our civic, social, and political life. I believe Christians in this country want to make a difference by preparing for and participating in the upcoming presidential election cycle, but we aren't always sure how to re-center ourselves, embrace our commitments with fresh clarity, and live as concerned and courageous people of faith. Once we do those things, we then can model for the wider community what disciplined, hopeful, just conversations look like. Together, we can lower the temperature and tension in the ecclesial and political system, while still focusing on what is at stake.

Honest conversations involve reflecting on our own part in the deterioration of our public discourse and policies. It also means we will muster courage to draw near to one another so that we can be close enough both to listen and confront. In the life of a Christian, as important as talking is, an honest conversation will lead to action, to constructive engagement that can help to purge the acerbic rhetoric and hateful action, and place us alongside one another as fellow citizens and purposeful agents of reconciliation, healing, and peace.

I know this sounds to some like a naïve fantasy. Even I recognize that it is beyond ambitious. What are the chances, really, of bringing together progressives and conservatives? Actually, though, I think that question highlights part of the problem.

Forget the progressive and conservative labels. They no longer apply. They reinforce the lazy prejudices of extremism rather than awaken us to a fresh moment with new friends. And besides, sometimes we can't support our own positions when using those labels, much less interpret them to others, or understand what others mean when they use them. To suggest that we can capture completely another person with these or any other label exacerbates the problem and thickens the fog in which we live.

While we're at it, let's forget the buzzwords that we stand behind. Let's come out from behind terms like family values and socialism and tree hugger and right wing. You tell me what matters to you and I'll tell you what matters to me. I am so confident of this opportunity that I'll refund what you paid for this book if you talk with someone from the "other side" and aren't surprised by how many common dreams and concerns you share with the person who only moments ago was your ignorant political enemy.

We also should abandon the notion that the debate can be framed by Democratic and Republican stances. Too much has changed and the political parties have not kept up. The disarray within all of them reveals that. The election of Donald Trump, whether you love him or despise him, resulted from self-preserving, unresponsive political parties lagging behind, often by several decades, instead of understanding the present and leading us into the future.

Turn a deaf ear to the shrill minority whose volume on issues is grossly disproportionate and unreasoned. They do not represent most Americans. Their jarring extremism cannot produce an environment that will bring people together. However, if all sides tone down their indignation for each other and dial back their rhetoric, a new day is possible for honest dialogue, deep understanding, fresh appreciation, imaginative solutions, and shared well-being.

And by all means, let's get real about the fact that with the exception of recording results on election night, the red state / blue state shorthand in most cases oversimplifies and disenfranchises whole groups of people. Presidential candidates shouldn't get away with only having to compete in a few swing states. What is true about the red state / blue state designations holds true for the church as well. There are many red churches and a few blue ones, but most churches are purple. Most congregations include a rich diversity of views and a range of commitments that enrich the whole. In other words, we don't have to draw people in to articulate a given position. Those people already participate in our congregations. Purple churches are well positioned to model discerning discussions on divisive topics, all the while sharing life together in worship, study, and service.[4]

Candidates and strategists nurture suspicion at every turn, but we need each other. We are fooling ourselves if we secretly believe that some of us in this country will thrive and the rest of us will fall away in failure and disgrace. To paraphrase President Lincoln, we will rise or fall together. Not everyone is convinced of that, and until we are, the future of our country is less bright.

My intent is neither to cheerlead or condemn in this book, but to urge the church to model for our villages, neighborhoods, and cities what honest, hopeful conversation can look like and what those conversations can achieve for the sake of ourselves and our neighbors, far and near. I vote every time I get the chance, including in every presidential election since I became age-eligible, but this is not a partisan book. One of the challenges in writing it is being confronted again with the reality that sometimes the best choice in a race is the least bad one, but that's democracy for you.

I occasionally hear or witness someone taking the lead in the effort to reset the rhetoric and refresh the political climate. For example, when President Trump, angered over a court's ruling on his administration's proposed asylum policy, slammed the decision made by "Obama judges," Chief Justice John Roberts broke his customary restraint to take exception to that comment. "We do not have Obama judges or Trump judges, Bush judges or Clinton judges," he said in a statement. "What we have is an extraordinary group of dedicated judges doing their level best to do equal right to those appearing before them. That independent judiciary is something we should all be thankful for."[5] I applaud Chief Justice

---

4. For a related and helpful resource, see Schade, *Preaching in the Purple Zone.*

5. Liptack, "Chief Justice Defends Judicial Independence."

Roberts's sentiment, even though it does not take into account the increasingly political dimension of judicial appointments.

But for the most part, I don't see many people able or willing to take the lead in this. I understand that. It will be risky. We will be vulnerable. But so much is at stake that thoughtful, compassionate Christians in this country need to do something, and naming the challenges and engaging the opportunities together is a start.

Many US congregations aren't as strong as they were even a few years ago, but it is time to go toward the action, not away from it. It will be hard because congregations are as anxious and depressed as much of the electorate. We are often unconvinced of the very things we say, sing, and pray in our worship. Many are trapped in vagueness and just trying to survive. We are also conflict avoidant, often intrigued by amusing and mildly fascinating religious ideas, but less inclined to make the core commitments of our faith visible and operational in our communities. Our mission statements may say otherwise, but a review of how we spend our time and allocate our resources signals that we focus more on our own comfort than on positive impact in the world.

But even if your congregation isn't as strong as it once was, perhaps you are more free now and less beholden to a culture that once co-opted our life and mission as Christians. I grew up benefitting from the culture's support of the church. The congregation of my youth was situated between a prominent bank and the county courthouse. The same people led all three institutions. It's humbling now to acknowledge that the culture's support of the church often moved us away from God's vision of shalom, not toward it. The absence of the culture's support has left us weaker in some respects, but freer in others, including for the conversations that I will describe in this book. This is about challenging what cannot stand, equipping for what matters most and bending the world toward the future that God desires.

## About This Book

This book is a collection of letters to the church. Each letter brings a biblical/theological perspective into conversation with a contemporary issue or situation. Questions for discussion are included at the end of each letter. You can read the book on its own, or take advantage of the discussion questions to use the book as the centerpiece for a Sunday School class, study group, retreat, or other engaging event.

I chose the ancient practice of letters because I am writing to my own sisters and brothers. I have spent my life in the church, including many years in parish ministry and now as a seminary professor. I love and appreciate the church. I also grow weary and disappointed with it. I hope people in congregations across the theological, sociopolitical, racial, ethnic, economic, and contextual spectrum will recognize both my love and disappointment and join me in constructive engagement to help bring about a new and fruitful season for all of us in this country.

The collection begins with a letter to ministers and a letter to congregations. You share in mutual vulnerability right now. Many of those relationships are strained and uncertain. Before launching into a broader conversation, I thought it would be helpful to offer thoughts on your particular roles and how you can renew your relationship and commitments.

The remainder of the letters are organized in three sections: The first section, entitled "What We Are Experiencing Now," describes some of the common thoughts and emotions that many Americans have expressed over the last few years. Sometimes, what we most need is for somebody to name what we are experiencing and to know that others are encountering something very similar. Otherwise, we may conclude that we have lost our senses and are stranded in isolation.

In the section entitled "What We Hope For," the letters describe some of the things worth desiring for our country. The list is far from exhaustive, of course, but the letters attempt to bring into focus some of the urgent matters and issues that are under debate—and seemingly under siege—when it comes to articulating what the character of our nation will be.

The third section of letters seeks to move all of us beyond the mode of a study group and into the arena of constructive engagement. The letters under the theme of "What We Are Called To" ask us to consider what we will do in order to bring about those things for which we hope.

The twenty letters are followed by a brief word entitled "Now That the Election Is Over." This book is going to press well before the general election season starts. Even though the US House of Representatives impeached Donald Trump in December 2019, he was declared not guilty by the US Senate, and it is almost certain that he will be the Republican nominee. Who the Democratic standard-bearer will be remains wildly unclear as I write this. Elections are significant markers in time. The democratic process that leads to the election or reelection of a president can be both fascinating and exasperating. Whatever the outcome of the 2020 presidential election, we will have enormous work to do as a country. This last letter of the book tries to send us on our way toward that work.

Again, the list of topics is far from exhaustive. I think engaging in the areas described in these letters will spur discussion that can lead to positive change, but I hope they also prompt you to think about other situations that cry out for healing, justice, and reconciliation. For some readers, this book won't go far enough in its criticism of certain political leaders and elected officials and you will be disappointed. For some, the reflections will go too far and you will be so offended that you put it down. I understand both of these responses, but my intent is not to give a political analysis or a campaign strategy. Nor, especially, is it to stoke further the anger and anxiety that so undercuts our ability to live together and talk and listen to each other.

My goal is help us think again about God's presence and purposes in our lives and in the world, to shine the light and language of our faith on issues and situations that threaten our common life, and to prompt us all to think about what it means to be the church in the face of these particular challenges and opportunities.

I hope the letters get your congregational conversation started in a helpful direction. If so, I am confident that your discussions, discoveries, and eventual engagement in the community will surpass the thought starters of these brief letters and lead you to model for all of us what difference a rigorous, reflective, hopeful conversation can make in the lives of its participants and in the life of the community of which you are part. You, no doubt, will raise important issues and critical situations that I have not addressed and, in the same way, think of ways to impact positively those issues and situations for the good of your community. I celebrate that. My desire simply is to get a conversation going that is too often dormant or irrelevant and to prompt you to unleash your voice, wisdom, talents, access, and passion on situations that cry out for your involvement. As that happens, the communities around us will take notice, learn from our example, and pursue the compassionate spirit and just policies that will benefit us all.

*1*

# A Letter to the Minister

Dear Friend in Ministry,

PASTORAL MINISTRY IS FULFILLING work. It's unlike nearly any other vocation or profession. We accompany people through seasons of confidence and doubt, often standing with them in their most exhilarating and heartbreaking moments. People trust us with their worries and dreams. They take comfort when we listen to them with care and then hold in prayer what they have shared with us.

Every week in worship we lead the faithful in the reenactment of our faith, a faith that once touched us so deeply that we began walking in the way of Jesus and later responded to a call to lead and serve the church. The church still sets aside time every week for our preaching and teaching. Not many in our society are allotted such an opportunity, but many of us get to do these things every week! While the talking heads sensationalize the day's events and issues, we offer encouragement and perspective when we proclaim the good news of God's love and justice for the whole world. We call people to take adventurous journeys of faith. We shepherd congregations through the sticky wickets of conflict and controversy and build up the body of Christ to be light and example to the world.

Ministry is scattered work at times, as you know. In between prayerfully studying the Scriptures, baptizing God's beloved, blessing the sick, and addressing inequity in the community come all those other things—the deficit in the church budget, asbestos in old floor tiles, repairs and updates of musical instruments, proper insurance documentation for the youth mission trip, and a dozen more. Some days, to quote Eugene Peterson, it can feel more like we are branch managers of a religious franchise than ministers guiding the church to be a sign of God's realm.[1]

I think the loss of trust in the church grows as much out of our own drift and distraction as out of conflict and controversy. Keeping the priorities and practices of the faith central to our own lives as ministers can pose a frequent challenge. Sustaining those priorities and practices at the heart of a congregation's life requires unusual stamina and focus. As the church, we too often turn inwardly upon ourselves and in doing so we turn away from the world into which we are sent to be peacemakers, ambassadors, reconcilers, and representatives. We spin our wheels in countless meetings and endless busy work, all the while failing to talk about anything very important because we may say something that will upset someone else in the room. The devotion "to the apostle's teaching and fellowship, to the breaking of bread and the prayers"[2] comes as an afterthought.

These days, however, we face something even more unmooring than drift and distraction, something that our busyness cannot solve and our technical fixes cannot address. If you are like most ministers I know, you feel less secure in your ministry position than you have in the past. The high anxiety, rigid views, and radioactive rhetoric have made their way into the church from the outside and many ministers feel vulnerable as a result. Some individual congregants quietly and unofficially have put pastors on notice, saying, "I am watching you."

I pray you are not serving in a congregation where people voice threats like these, but even apart from their explicit expression, it is still a very vulnerable time. Our country is emotionally charged and politically divided and we can't expect people to leave

1. Peterson, *Pastor*, 119.
2. Acts 2:42.

their opinions, anxiety, and anger at the church door. People are carefully adjusting their antennas to pick up on anything from the pulpit or the lectern that sounds even remotely partisan. Some are ready to pounce on the preacher, the church school teacher, the chair of the deacons, the guest presenter, and even their oldest friend at the first sound of a critique of an officeholder they support, the political party to which they belong, or a policy with which they agree. It can be difficult to find passages when Jesus and his early followers were not criticizing and condemning the Roman Empire for its economic disparity and political violence, but apparently in some churches that should not make its way into our preaching and teaching.

I want to believe we can find and embrace some good news in this. In some cases, it may only be one person who is attempting to censor your sermons or lessons. That doesn't lessen the feeling of being at risk, especially if you suspect the one person may hold political sway in the congregation, but it does mean that the rest of the congregation can rise up to model and nurture a more open and discerning spirit. At times, it may take more than this. I know that these threats are made by people who are anxious and volatile themselves, but the congregation may need to confront and help people channel their rage and fear constructively.

And there's more good news here. It's a wonderful thing to have people on the edge of their seats and listening so closely! Not only is that much preferred to people slumping in apathy and yawning at the gospel as if it is yesterday's news, but isn't this kind of attention the very thing we have wanted? Haven't we longed for people to lean into the moment and hungrily engage the Scriptures? With all that is going on in our world, it's exciting and hopeful if people in this time really want to know if there is any word from the Lord. As people lean in, we are left to decide whether we also will lean into this moment to listen afresh for what matters to us and to commit anew to living those gospel values in the midst of the congregations we lead.

So, for what feels like an insecure time for some, I offer these three words of encouragement. First, ministry happens through the hard work of developing trusting relationships. Unfortunately, the uncertainty and anxiety that people in your church are feeling can place a strain on even the best of relationships. A lot has changed and people are trying to navigate the loss and grief. Sometimes, people direct their anger at you because at some level they view you as the safest outlet.

Many topics never get raised for fear of undue suspicion and attack. Holidays may have always been tricky, but now soccer matches and birthday parties carry the same uncertainty and tension. It's as if Jesus' words have come true: "One household will be divided, three against two and two against three; they will be divided: father against son and son against father, mother again daughter and daughter against mother"[3] and so on.

In this kind of tense, divisive environment, we may find ourselves looking for safe spaces and safe conversation partners, but the sometimes risky atmosphere does not change the truth of this statement—ministry happens through relationships. We cannot share life together in any meaningful, joyful way apart from relationships built on trust. Relationships develop and deepen through our presence, honesty, vulnerability, and fidelity to each other. Good experience in these relationships over time will help to lower the tension so that we can listen to each other, understand the concerns being voiced, and draw on the strength of the relationship. So, even though you may be tempted by the idea of shelter and seclusion, the way forward, now more than ever, is to continue to develop and sustain trusting, purposeful relationships.

Second, I encourage you to remember that people want something from their church experience. We cannot provide everything that some people will want, but church can still be a rich experience for those seeking God, longing for meaning, wrestling with questions, and seeking connection. When my family and I go to church, we see Never-Trumpers and Trump enthusiasts, pro-choice and pro-life advocates, and people of various races, ethnicities, nationalities, classes, sexual orientations, and gender identities, but all of us have come to church for something more

3. Luke 12:52–52.

than the single label that sometimes gets attached to us. I believe people want to be part of a greater story and church provides that. We go to church not only to express what matters to us, but to learn what should matter to us as followers of Jesus, worshippers of a just and holy God, and members of the human race.

And I think people come to be inspired. We are drowning in information, some of it totally baseless. We are running woefully short on inspiration. We know we can be and do better. We know that a welcoming community of honesty and encouragement is possible. We know we can make a difference in the community around us. In many cases, we already have the gifts and skills to impact situations positively, but we're not always inspired to get involved in any deep way. Church can be an important place for people to experience that inspiration.

Third, please remember that the church has authorized you to do certain things. It's true that ministry happens through relationships, but in this pastor-congregation relationship, the church has authorized you to preach the gospel, to lead the faithful in worship, to care for people in distress, to shepherd the congregation through opportunities and challenges and to represent Christ and the church to the world. Either through your ordination vows or the terms of your call or your job description, the church has given you this authority. We may wish for more status, power, and security, but we already have the authorization that we seek. We might wish for a different position from which to do this work, but the pastoral role offers a wonderful platform to do the ministry the church has given us to do.

We live in a hyper-critical time, which means it is even more the case that we will encounter conflict, endure criticism, and fall out of favor with some people whose esteem we value, but not every disagreement is persecution and not every misunderstanding is terminal. The trusting relationships with our congregants reaffirm the authority we have been given to preach faithfully, teach soundly, lead worship inspiringly, and care for people prayerfully. All of this fosters an environment where people can appreciate the complementary nature of differences and live well together as the community of Jesus Christ.

I hope something here is helpful for you and your ministry. Perhaps what I most want you to know is that I honor you and I celebrate your ministry. And just as I have frequent reminders of people praying for me, so I will be praying for you, your church, and this world God loves so much.

Your friend in ministry,
Bill

## 2

# A Letter to the Congregation

Dear People of God,

WE ALL HAVE OUR beliefs, impressions, and experiences of church. Just saying the word *church* conjures all sorts of different perspectives and ideas. For some, church means acceptance and healing. Others have come away from church wounded and confused. Some will point to how church connects to their everyday lives. Others will report that they cannot think of a more irrelevant organization or a more boring experience.

Congregations display a mix of major differences and less consequential ones. For example, an Orthodox priest functions very differently compared to a Southern Baptist pastor. Drums and guitars can be found in some sanctuaries, while in others the pipe organ and a grand piano prominently occupy the sacred space. Whether a congregation is aligned with a denominational family often signals certain commitments and values. In some churches, prohibiting anyone from participating in Communion is an abomination. In others, historical practices and doctrinal claims support the exclusion from the Eucharist for anyone not yet confirmed in that tradition.

Some traditions celebrate the ordination of women, but not all. In recent years, more traditions have welcomed LGBTQ persons fully into the life and leadership of the church, but many do not. All of these examples represent major differences in how various parts of the body of Christ live out what it means to be the church. For every major difference, dozens of less important ones come into play that reflect trends and local culture. Of course, adjudicating what is a major or a minor difference often can lead to tension and conflict. I think what people wear to church is a fairly minor issue, but I know of people who rank church attire as one of the most important dimensions of the faith.

It's not easy these days to be the church. It's important to stand back from the American religious landscape and note that some churches of various sizes, worship styles, denomination (or no denomination), and location are doing quite well, but many are struggling. Many of our churches are smaller than they used to be. They find themselves on uncertain financial footing and exerting less influence in the wider community. The anxiety and contentiousness of our culture creeps into church life and further complicates the work of being the church.

And yet, we are still called and expected by God to be the church. The church is the eschatological community of Christ. That often gets lost amid all the other local customs, organizational obsessions, group dynamics, agendas, and idiosyncrasies that swirl about in a congregation. We are an eschatological community, so what does that mean?

Eschatology refers to end things, to the ultimate destiny of the world and its people. For Christians, eschatology expresses the belief and hope that the ways of God will prevail upon the earth. Scripture describes this vision in various ways. For example, the powerful image of the peaceable realm in Isaiah 11 concludes with this vision: "They will not hurt or destroy on all my holy mountain; for the earth will be full of the knowledge of the Lord as the waters cover the sea."[1]

Another image comes from Jesus' comparing the kingdom of heaven to a great banquet at which all the children of God will

1. Isa 11:9.

feast, including those marginalized and oppressed in this life.[2] The Lord's Supper is a foretaste of that heavenly banquet.

Still another image comes from the Revelation to John, the last book in the New Testament. The eschatological vision announced in the closing chapters offers this promise: "See, the home of God is among mortals. He will dwell with them; they will be his peoples, and God himself will be with them; he will wipe every tear from their eyes. Death will be no more; mourning and crying and pain will be no more, for the first things have passed away. And the one who was seated on the throne said, 'See, I am making all things new.'"[3] In short, eschatology proclaims that God's promises will be fulfilled.

For the church to be an eschatological community means that we are living already with these promises and by these promises. The church is not the realm or kingdom of God, though it claimed that position for many centuries, but we are the community that points always to God's realm and even now we embody God's good future for creation and humanity. In the church, we embody God's promises now, in advance of the ultimate fulfillment of those promises. We don't just say, "Thy will be done," we seek to live the ways of God and continue the work of Jesus in the world. We offer ourselves humbly to the world as an alternative community that participates in God's preferred future. In worship, we enact God's life-giving story, each time claiming the future promises of God for the present moment. In fact, the image of the church portrayed in Ephesians is that the world should be able to see the wisdom and work of God by examining the life of the church.[4]

And yet, not always. At least not yet and not fully. We in the church can become distracted, shortsighted, and disconnected from the life to which God calls us. We fail to model God's promises to the world around us and sometimes to each other in the church. Our language can grow coarse while our attitudes deteriorate and our prejudices rage. We draw boundaries around God's

2. Luke 14:5–24; Matt 22:1–14.
3. Rev 21:3–5a
4. Eph 3:10.

realm at our country's borders, or at a particular issue, and sometimes even at our own church's walls and doors. We often cannot seem to show up as our best, grace-filled selves and, as a result, the church is experienced as narrow, rigid, and downright mean.

This is the tension with which we live. We point to God's presence and purposes, but often do not or cannot fulfill them ourselves, at least not yet and not fully. So, just as I did in the letter to your minister, I offer these words of encouragement.

First, I encourage you to lift your sights beyond the organizational side of church with all its meetings, building concerns, and efforts to fill slots and positions and consider what it would look like for your congregation to be an eschatological community of God's presence and purposes. We will still need to meet, plan, and tend to some basic needs that every organization faces, but what would it look like for your congregation to shift its focus so that your first priority is to model for the world around you the grace, joy, reconciliation, and peace of God?

Paul urged the Philippians, "Let the same mind be in you that was in Christ Jesus."[5] He described that mind of Christ as one of encouragement, love, joy, humility, and goodwill toward others. Imagine the compelling witness the church would be if we modeled those things to each other and to our communities.

Instead, too many view the church as out of touch, a place of rampant in-fighting and division, complicit in structural racism and sexism, and concerned only with its own survival. In that same letter, Paul asks the church in Philippi to take note of what is true, honorable, just, pure, pleasing, commendable, and all things excellent, but not just to create a study group around those things. No, in a bold statement, Paul asks the Philippians to do those things—to be a community of Jesus Christ with truth, honor, justice, purity, and excellent things at the very center of its life.[6]

Second, I hope you will cherish your church experience. That includes cherishing what feeds your spirit and cherishing those in the congregation who are making the journey of faith with you.

5. Phil 2:5.
6. Phil 4:8–9.

Paul used the Greek word *koinonia* to describe the fellowship of the church. It is the same word he used to describe the Lord's Supper, which reminds us of how holy the source is of our relationships with each other.[7] We are sisters and brothers who continue to be open to God's spirit and to offer our gifts and graces to cultivate the kind of community I describe above. It's not easy work. We grow tired of each other at times. We throw sharp elbows now and then and even sharper words. In some cases, we don't know each other very well and, in other cases, we've been together so long in the same church that we know each other all too well!

It's risky to give ourselves again and again to the making of the beloved community. We already feel vulnerable enough these days without opening ourselves to more uncertainty and fresh disappointment, but we do not and cannot become partners in the gospel by keeping our distance and maintaining our defensiveness. Our openness to the Spirit and to each other becomes the catalyst by which we discover and enjoy the depths of joy and purpose the faith of the church holds.

Third, I encourage you to value your minister's work. I personally know the difference this makes. I served congregations in a variety of settings. They shared a lot of things in common, but they also faced some unique opportunities and challenges. I tried to shepherd those congregations in a faithful direction, though I know that many times my shepherding was modest at best. And sometimes, no doubt, I didn't lead us in the most faithful direction possible, which is a humbling thing to look back on now.

What I know is this: the weeks and months when the congregation voiced its support made many more things possible and far more enjoyable. That does not mean the congregation always needs to agree with the minister and that is not what I am referring to here. In fact, many times the way I experienced the congregation's support occurred through conversation and debate that reframed the issue and refined our plans. The greatest support that I experienced came through the congregation's active involvement in building up the body of Christ in that place. In those moments,

7. Phil 1:3; 1 Cor 10:16.

I trusted that the church supported me in what it had authorized me to do and I always will be grateful for that. I hope you will offer that kind of involvement and partnership to your minister.

And I hope these words help all of us be the church in these times of tension, division, and uncertainty. As Paul said to the Philippians,

I thank my God every time I remember you,[8]
Bill

8. Phil 1:3.

# What We Are Experiencing Now

## 3

# Often On Edge and Off Balance

My Sisters and Brothers,

BEING ON EDGE AND off balance is no way to live. We do not function well as individuals when we are anxious. When the systems around us that are intended to provide stability and support receive a daily infusion of uncertainty, it causes those systems to create an enveloping emotional uncertainty that can manipulate everyone in its reach.

Anxious systems no longer work for us, but rather decenter us from what we know and trust. They seek to control our identity, thoughts, actions, and loyalties. They know that if they can control us they will keep us from calling things what they are. If we are always nervous, that nervousness will cause us to turn inwardly upon ourselves, thus allowing whatever dumb, mean, or unethical idea to proceed without our notice or objection.

It's an awful way to lead. It violates trust, creates unnecessary uncertainty, and sets groups against one another, but leaders do it because they know it works. Were it not so inhumane and unproductive, it would be a brilliant political strategy!

Many enthusiastic supporters of President Trump tell me that they just wish he would stop tweeting and talking because, in their view, some of his policies improve situations. Instead, though, we are left to wonder, will the next tweet demean a whole segment of the American population? Will the next post reveal that the talks with another of the world's nuclear powers are spiraling out of control? Will the next notification announce another round of family separations at the US-Mexico border?

What situation will be caricatured beyond recognition in the next tweet? What political opponent will be destroyed in today's campaign rally? What established policies will be called into question with the next off-the-cuff comment?

## Why This Issue Matters

Sometimes just naming the issue aloud refreshes our perspective and calms our spirits. These days, there's a lot of naming to do when it comes to our country's anxiety. Newsfeeds come at us at all hours and with few clues about how to sort through them for what is important. It takes considerable effort to recognize whether a news story announces a new policy, reverses an existing one, or creates a distraction to divert our attention away from something officials do not want us to see. Leaders and media outlets bombard us with information that is designed to deepen our anxiety and to leverage it for political gain. This feeling of too often being on edge leads to an anxiety that threatens to discourage and paralyze us.

No wonder we are so anxious, but before saying anything else let's pause to clarify what we are talking about and experiencing. I am not referring to anxiety in the clinical sense. Individuals who struggle with any degree of an anxiety disorder face particular needs that warrant the involvement of a mental health counselor and, sometimes, medication. I am not qualified to address this kind of anxiety. I can only imagine how the anxiety afoot in today's political and cultural climate can complicate severely the challenges of an anxiety disorder. For those dealing with an anxiety disorder, I am deeply sorry for your pain and I offer my hope and prayers for good care and less anxious days.

The anxiety to which I am referring impacts us whether we have an individual anxiety disorder or not. It envelopes us like a fog and, much like a fog, the cause of this pervasive anxiety is often difficult to define and address. I am referring to the anxiety that operates in an emotional system where we are all connected to each other, even if we don't know each other and do not move in the same physical space.

We are all part of such systems and feel their emotional force. In a family, it's hard to think of something that impacts one person that doesn't also impact the rest of the family emotionally in some way. The pastor is anxious, and so the church is also. The president of the school or the company or the country is anxious and their anxiety spreads through those systems. In all these cases, the emotional calmness or rashness of a few key people spreads through the system. Only those with a determined ability to differentiate themselves from those emotional waves can maintain their own identity and keep the system moving in a helpful direction. We attempt that differentiation while we deal with our own emotions, motivations, loyalties, fears, and disappointments. In other words, we all function as individual systems while we live and make the best of the bigger systems of which we are part.

It gives me no joy that I am emotionally connected to Donald Trump, Nancy Pelosi, and Mitch McConnell, but I am. Why else would I jump and cringe at the latest headline and the most recent news conference? It's true that I also jump and cringe at various pronouncements and decisions because I care about the people who will be adversely affected by certain policies and actions and because I worry about the character and future of our country, but the anxiety in a system is always more than one decision or action. It falls to me to set, as best as I can, my own emotional temperature in order to give me the best chance of keeping my balance and living from my truest center.

We know the system is supposed to function in a much more thoughtful, beneficial way. Ideally, we elect women and men who can exercise their imagination and courage on behalf of the well-being of us all. And thankfully, a few gifted and wise people continue to seek public office. When the system allows, they bring their passion, ideas, solutions and collaboration to bear on various opportunities and many intractable challenges.

However, working things through the current political system is very difficult. The pace of cultural and technological change continues to accelerate and governmental leadership does not rise to the needed levels of insight, political will, and effectiveness. If the system is not broken, it is at least terribly in need of an overhaul. In a democracy, we are the ones who must demand the overhaul, even though anxiety may grip us at times. The system will not reform on its own. There are simply too many benefits for those within the system for the changes to occur without sustained pressure from outside the system.

## The Witness of the Church

We are often anxious and afraid, but we are not helpless, not as individuals, the country, or the church. To use the Apostle Paul's phrase, we know there is "a more excellent way"[1] to live and lead as the church than to keep people on edge and off balance. The way of love does not manipulate people or information for its own benefit, but rather assures us that we have an identity and a purpose grounded in God's love for us. The certainty of God's presence among us allows us to step back, to breathe, to remember who and whose we are, to reclaim our lives, and to shine light on situations mired in anxiety. The lively, consistent celebration and experience in a congregation of God's loving presence creates an emotional, spiritual, physical space that re-centers us as the beloved. Through hymns, prayers, Scripture, and the Sacred Meal, we connect with a story that fosters deep peace and community, thus allowing us to know ourselves and each other again as God's own. We find the desired intimacy with God and one another in community, while at the same time nurturing the individual distance and identity we need to rediscover what we value and cherish.

1. 1 Cor 12:31.

Once re-centered, the light of Christ in us brings the world back into focus from the anxiety that distorted it. The light of Christ prompts us to ask important questions about motives and situations and to see the way of Jesus in all things. The light of Christ in us exposes the efforts to keep us on edge and off balance for what they are—attempts to define and limit us with anxiety— but the gospel is that only God defines who we are.

We are God's own, loved without exception or limit. God calls us to stand back and take a fresh look at ourselves as the beloved, and then to look out on the world with fresh eyes, a new heart and the light of Christ.

I find the image of a balcony to be a particularly helpful one.[2] Imagine going to a mental, spiritual, and emotional place that provides distance from anxiety's tentacles and hooks, free from the day's worries and tasks. On that balcony, you take some deep breaths and look down to view your own life and the life of your family, church, and country. There you become disentangled from the narratives that seek to control, confine, and limit you. You see inhibiting and wasteful patterns prevailing from which you want to separate yourself. You identify things you want to let go of now, knowing you have carried them too long.

You see with new appreciation the many good things that are happening around you. You hear, as if you have never heard these words before, Jesus speaking: "Do not let your hearts be troubled. Believe in God, believe also in me . . . Peace I leave with you; my peace I give to you."[3]

The invitation comes to you to accept God's definition for you, to live afresh as the beloved, to rise and focus and act, to choose life, to dare to choose life, even if no one else around you can do that yet.

Still on the balcony, still becoming reacquainted with God's boundless love and hopeful calling, you see the playfulness and joy that are possible. You open your life to dreaming and learning, to shed the overbearing seriousness that marks an anxious emotional

2. Heifetz, *Leadership without Easy Answers*, 252.

3. John 14:1, 18, 27.

system, to demonstrate the calm focus that allows confident engagement with each other, with the world and with God.

We reenter our lives, bringing with us all we experienced on the balcony. Our calm and confidence spread through our emotional systems instead of the anxiety that did previously. We begin to experience church as a truly generative fellowship where we access anew the life-giving dimension of our faith story.

Now we turn toward the world that God loves so much. Not a lot has changed with the world while we were on the balcony, but we have changed, even if only for today. Even if we have to return to the balcony again tomorrow to re-center again.

The anxiety does not define us. We are God's beloved, blessed by God to be a blessing to others.

Yours in the peace of Christ,
Bill

## Questions for Discussion

1. What are the main sources of anxiety in America and how does the current time compare in anxiety to previous times?

2. In addition to gaining perspective from getting on an imaginary balcony, how else do you rise above anxiety and maintain a calm, focused, and playful presence as individuals and as the church?

3. If not by keeping us on edge and off balance, how do you want leaders at all levels of public life to lead and how will that shape your thinking as you consider your votes for various races in the 2020 US election?

# 4

# A Craving for Certainty

My Sisters and Brothers,

WHEN WE ARE ANXIOUS, we crave certainty. It's a natural and understandable response. We all do it to some degree. We look for
things in our lives and world about which we can be sure. We seek
to eliminate as many variables as possible and pin down as many
safe bets as we can. When we are anxious, we do not have the emotional stamina or the intellectual curiosity to tolerate ambiguity
well. When we are anxious, we find it very difficult to tolerate the
gray areas of our own lives, much less those of our nation's politics.
Situations that can only be described as "on the one hand / on the
other hand" frustrate and weary us when we are already having
trouble sorting things out. If we hear of one more "fluid situation"
or another "unsettled matter," we think we will scream.

At our most anxious, we not only look for certainty, we crave
it and we cling to it, even if we have to suspend much of what we
otherwise know and trust in order to do so.

Do you remember the story of the golden calf in Exodus 32?
The people waited and waited on Moses to come down the mountain with the tablets of the covenant. The wait probably seemed
worth it at first. After all, what could be more reassuring and

clarifying than hearing from Moses about what God expected and wanted for the people?

But at some point the grumbling started. "Who knows what happened to Moses? He may not even be coming back. We need something now, something we can count on!" So Aaron, who apparently had absorbed the people's anxiety rather than regulating his own, grew a little impatient. The open-endedness of the situation got the best of him and he gave in. "Bring me all your gold rings and, like our neighbors of the region often do, I'll mold them into the golden calf, build an altar, and call a festival." Aaron appears to have been so caught up in the people's anxiety and his own discomfort that he not only initiates the flash festival, he even credits the golden calf with liberating people from their slavery in Egypt! That's right. Aaron invoked the most significant narrative in the life of God's people and then assigned the liberating power of that story not to God, but to a molten calf that didn't exist even a few minutes before.

God was not amused, but we can understand what the people were experiencing. We know well the vulnerability of those uncertain moments. It stops us in our tracks. We look for things to steady us. We crave nearly any form of reassurance that we aren't as close to the cliff as it feels like we are and we're not as helpless as other people want us to believe. The open-ended nature of most of life leaves too much unsettled at a time when we want to nail things down. The faster things change the less sense we can make of them.

## Why This Issue Matters

As humans, we long for certain things, like trusting relationships, meaningful lives, and a loving, guiding hand in the midst of life's events and surprises. We also long for security. In fact, security may be our primary longing, at least at times. Little else is possible without it.

The last thing we want to face with any regularity is our own finitude. We will do most anything to avoid acknowledging our limitations. This isn't to say that we are lacking in possibilities, gifts, and agency, but we are finite beings. Ever since our eyes were opened in Eden to the joys and sorrows, the good and evil of human life, we have been acquainted, sometimes all too painfully, with our limits. The Letter of James startles us with its bluntness: "For you are a mist that appears for a little while and then vanishes."[1]

We approach our limits in different ways. Some work night and day to disprove the limits of the human condition, brashly denying that those limits and rules apply to them. Others will fall into despair and depression at the thought that, as James put it, we are but a mist. I admit that is not a verse around which I build my morning devotion!

Still others respond to this humbling news by looking around and identifying things that we can cling to in order to ease our anxiety. This is what Aaron and the people did and we do it, too. All of us participate in this idol-making to some degree. The difference is whether we recognize at the time what we are doing and acknowledge the misplaced loyalties and skewed perspectives that inevitably flow from our own golden calf efforts.

Our craving for certainty can shape our understanding of God in profound ways. When anxiety is high and our search for certainty is underway, we start looking for a supreme power who can fix things, who can bring order back into our lives, and often, who will exact revenge on those individuals and groups whom we deem to be the source of disruption, chaos, and deterioration. We fashion ourselves a god who will "repay you for the years the swarming locust has eaten,"[2] though we usually refer to our political enemies and social adversaries as things far worse than swarming locusts. In Scripture, we find just enough evidence of that kind of deity and then we fill in the rest of the picture in ways that benefit us. We sometimes pray for the Day of the Lord with the assumption that our enemies will suffer their final defeat while we will be exalted and our agendas will be confirmed. It doesn't

---

1. Jas 4:14.
2. Joel 2:25.

always occur to us that, as Archbishop Tutu puts it, our enemies may not be God's enemies.[3]

Simply put, we often make idols out of our positions on social issues, religious practice, the political parties with which we affiliate, and in how we assign divine sanction to our own country's actions without coupling that with any critique of our polices at home and our involvement in the world. Then, when we are anxious, we deploy these idols as signs that we hold the ultimate truth. We hope their certainty can help us regain what is missing from our lives. We can even use our idols as weapons against each other, but more than anything we use them to attempt to calm our own anxiety and fear. It makes me ask, what do we fear seeing or hearing? What do we fear encountering and addressing?

## The Witness of the Church

What if we, as people of faith, approached our limits in a different way? What if, instead of certainty, we sought to live well and authentically with our limitations rather than pretend that those limitations do not exist? Jesus promised that he came so that we could know and experience abundant life.[4] He was not naïve or confused about the finite nature of human life. In fact, he offers abundant life in direct contrast to a thief who steals and destroys. Jesus believed that in the midst of the limits, we can live hopefully, joyfully, and compellingly. This is our story. More than that, this is our promise and our witness as Christians.

Imagine what changes if, instead of dashing to our corners with our hardline positions and headstrong accusations, we move toward each other. Imagine what changes if, instead of demanding that others bow down to our favorite golden calf, we gather around a table with one another, acknowledge each other's presence, practice deep listening for what matters to each of us, and learn why it is so important to us.

---

3. Tutu, *God Has a Dream*, 49–50.

4. John 10:10.

This is our story and practice as Christians. The more we model it the more those in the wider community will take note of it and begin to practice it. If, though, we persist in our self-absorption, triviality, and infighting, we will not bear witness to the promise of gathering together and the world around us will dismiss us for our irrelevance.

Imagine what changes if, instead of hurling tweets at each other and further hyperventilating the country, we recover not the art of the deal, but the commitment to civil conversation and the art of constructive dialogue. Our country is a presence and an experience worth sustaining, even with our sins and shortcomings, but we will not live into our next great era if we do not commit to heartfelt conversations, broad inclusion, real debate, prayerful discernment, and productive compromise.

Again, this is the church's story. We have not always handled it as prayerfully and kindly as we could have, but the Christian story has evolved over two thousand years through faithful retelling, by making claims about the life to which God calls us, and then living those claims with neighbors far and near.

Imagine what changes if, instead of anointing one person to be "the chosen one," as former cabinet member Rick Perry and others have done of President Trump, we reinvigorate our faith and our citizenship to believe that any future goodness and greatness of the United States depends on all of us sharing in the work. Imagine what changes if, instead of further empowering a single, anxiety-ridden person, we reclaim the power of the ballot to support those who work to bring the country together rather than deliberately dividing and polarizing us against each other.

If Christians are less anxious than the rest of the country these days, it is barely the case. We are certainly not without our blind spots when it comes to producing and celebrating idols, only to learn how they diminish us with their rigidity, exclusion, and impotence. And so, we travel by faith and not by sight.[5] It's a journey that involves honesty and humility, knowing that we can neither eliminate uncertainty nor become captives to things that

5. 2 Cor 5:7.

hold no real comfort or guidance. And all along the way, God is present and God is faithful.

That is the walk of faith and I imagine that it can and will bear fruit when we most need it.

Your hopeful fellow traveler,
Bill

## Questions for Discussion

1. What idols do you believe most tempt Americans and how can your faith help you understand and deal with that temptation?

2. For those times and things about which we cannot be certain, what does "walking by faith" mean to you and what does that look like in your life as individuals and as the church?

3. How do you want to see candidates balance the need for some certainty with the need to walk sometimes by faith and how will that shape your thinking as you consider your votes for various races in the 2020 US election?

# 5

# People Reduced to a Single Dimension

My Sisters and Brothers,

ALL PEOPLE BEAR THE *imago Dei*, the image of God. We are wonderfully made in God's image and carry that divine stamp as God's own. But that doesn't mean we always notice it in each other or even in ourselves. Lately, it seems, we barely disguise the fact that we no longer are looking with the intent of seeing each other in this way. To see the image of God in each other involves pausing wherever we are, whatever we are doing, and looking with openness upon each other to see the wonder and beauty that we all carry.

The truth is that we do not see each other. Not often enough. Not really. Not in the most helpful ways. When it comes time to understand and size someone up, we turn to the easiest, quickest way of doing so. We reduce the person to a single dimension or label or category and move on to something else.

And sometimes, God help us, we cover over that divine image in each other and in ourselves to the point that we no longer see each other or ourselves as God's own. That happens out in the world and it happens in our own families and in the church.

Dr. Gregory Ellison is on a mission to change that. Ellison teaches at a seminary in Atlanta and came to our school to speak a couple of years ago. You know how these public lectures go—someone introduces the speaker, the speaker makes the perfunctory remark that "it's good to see you today," and then the speaker launches into the lecture.

But that's not the way this lecture began. Our dean introduced Ellison and he came on stage, but he didn't say anything. Instead, he went from person to person to person, looking every person in the room directly in the eye. You can imagine how this might work in a room of eight to ten people. The dead air would be a little awkward, but the charade would be over soon enough. In this case, though, Ellison was speaking—or eventually would be—in our auditorium and it was packed. We watched in silence, all 425 of us, as Ellison went person to person, row by row, section by section, until he had seen each and every one of us. And only then did he begin talking.

You probably are trying to picture this in your mind.[1] Maybe you are so accurately imagining this scene that you are feeling some of the discomfort and awkwardness that accompanied the opening moments of his lecture. Could he not have offered at the beginning the usual blanket statement "It's good to see you" to the whole group that most speakers rattle off without much thought or meaning?

He could have, but Ellison says that nothing changes until we really see each other. I believe that now in ways that I did not before. I felt something changing in the room that day as Ellison went from person to person, row to row, section to section. I believe some people went from feeling invisible to feeling seen that day as Ellison made his way through that large room.

Ellison has been doing this since 2013 when he began the initiative Fearless Dialogues.[2] Since then, thousands of people on four continents have participated in this project, but don't be fooled by its title into thinking that a fearless dialogue begins with

---

1. To see a video of Ellison opening a lecture in this way, go to "MTS Barbara Holmes Lecture: Rev. Dr. Greg Ellison II's Fearless Dialogues," YouTube video, 1:19:07, posted March 22, 2019, https://www.youtube.com/watch?v=-zDg-LnbJo8.

2. https://www.fearlessdialogues.com/.

talking or even listening. No, a fearless dialogue begins with seeing. In a fearless dialogue, we get close enough to each other to catch more than a glance. We are close enough and still enough to see the very image of God in each other.

## Why This Issue Matters

We too frequently size people up with a single dimension—Democrat, Republican, pro-choice, pro-life, gay, straight, and whatever other labels, categories, and single dimensions we can use to define someone for our own convenience. We mostly want to be able to say that we noticed that person before moving on, even if it was just a glance from a distance.

Brené Brown says, "People are hard to hate close up. Move in."[3] Until we see each other there are no fearless dialogues, only the defaults of prior conversations and distanced judgments. We will remain to each other the immigrant, the Washington insider, the white Southerner, the urban poor, the incarcerated black man, the techie, the Millennial, and so on, and we'll organize our worldview around categories like these for our own convenience, comfort, and privilege.

Not seeing each other allows us to do awful things to each other without understanding or having to account for the damage. We not only diminish the divine image in others by doing so, we also diminish ourselves. Wonder and beauty do not come alive in us as long as we refuse to see it in others. We cannot know the exhilaration of wonder and beauty as long as we boil down the glory God has stamped on us all to a single dimension devoid of promise and surprise.

We spend a lot of time side by side at school in prearranged classrooms and at homes in matching chairs in front of the television. In the church, most sanctuaries are designed so that what we see most often is the back of someone else's head. Even when we are across the dinner table from each other, we look past each

3. Brown, *Braving the Wilderness*, 36.

other or through each other, swiping pages on our devices and moving food from one side of our plate to the other.

When we don't see each other, we do not know each other. When we don't see each other, we don't trust each other. When we don't see or know or trust each other, we don't work well together on projects and problems. And when we don't see each other, it's no wonder we don't hear each other, talk with each other, connect with each other, dream with each other, lament with each other, collaborate with each other, and problem-solve with each other.

It can be hard to look into the eyes of someone we don't know, or someone whom we perceive to be different from us, or, and this is the really tough one, someone we know but with whom either the relationship has grown stale or we have a serious conflict. It can be breathtaking to look at someone, to really see someone up close, and know their disappointment and pain by what we see in their eyes. And so we back away, lest seeing someone else's pain brings up our own.

## The Witness of the Church

Do you remember the story of the Pharisee and the tax collector in Luke 18?[4] One day they both went up to the temple to pray—the Pharisee with his sacred studies and rituals and the tax collector as the despised colluder with the Roman government. And remember, they were there to pray, but I wonder what would have been different if they had seen each other.

The tax collector offered no pedigree or credentials. He prayed, throwing himself on the mercy of God, and left. As happens with all of us, the Pharisee seems to have lost his focus at some point. Instead of lifting up his head and heart to God in prayer, he looked sideways at the tax collector, but only long enough to size him up and move on. "Thank you, God, that I am not like this tax collector."

The Pharisee was aware of the tax collector's presence, but I don't think he saw the humanity of the tax collector. I don't think

4. Luke 18:9–14.

he saw any of this man's life beyond that label. The Pharisee may have looked in the tax collector's general direction, but it takes more than a glance to really see someone. The Pharisee relied on a single dimension, that of being a tax collector, to size up the man and dismiss him.

I wonder what would have been different if the Pharisee and the tax collector had seen each other. Not just there at the temple, but in the rest of their lives and in the community. What if, instead of a glance, instead of operating with convenient labels, these two would see each other, really see each other, up close? What if they moved beyond the single dimension that had been assigned to the other, beyond the default groupings used to categorize one another, and beyond hurry or custom or laziness that kept those labels in place? And I wonder what would be different for us, you know, if we really saw each other.

I should have known what was coming that day at the end of Ellison's lecture. He asked us to pair up with someone nearby. Warren and I didn't really know each other, though we have served on a few school and community committees together over the years, but there we stood—nose to nose and toes and to toes.

Ellison continued his directions. "Say to the person right in front of you, 'It's nice to see you,' and then spend the next two minutes seeing the person and making observations about what you see."

"Two minutes! Are you serious?" I'm going to wager that not very many lovers look upon each other for two minutes without interruption. It's a terribly vulnerable thing to do.

I described the contours of Warren's face, the grays and blacks of his beard, the color of his eyes. I believe he felt like I had seen him. I felt seen as well when it was his turn to see me for two minutes and to make similar observations. We had never really seen each other before. Doing so in that moment changed our relationship.

This is the gospel: we are marvelously made—all of us![5] We bear the image of the Creator. All of us. And that divine image

5. Ps 139:14 MSG.

holds more wonder and beauty than we can capture or describe. We cannot reduce it to a singular dimension or label or stereotype, try as we might with our meanness and ignorance, our avoidance and conflict and our dastardly political strategies. The wonder and beauty persist. They are always present for our seeing. They are always ready to open a new future to us.

Hoping to see you soon,
Bill

## Questions for Discussion

1. How does your faith cause you to really see, appreciate, and care for people who to this point have remained unknown and perhaps even invisible to you?

2. In what ways do you want local, state, and national leaders to affirm the dignity of every human being and how will that priority shape your thinking as you consider your votes for various races in the 2020 US election?

3. Pair up with someone. One of you begin by saying, "It's good to see you," then look upon the other person for two minutes and make observations about what you see of the person before you. Then switch roles and repeat.

4. What did you learn about the other person in doing this?

5. What did you learn about yourself?

6. What did you learn about the value and importance of seeing?

7. How will that translate into action in your community and world?

# 6

# The Revival of Deadly Prejudices

My Sisters and Brothers,

ON THE DAY AFTER an assassin killed Dr. King in Memphis, I was playing in my backyard with a second-grade classmate named Steve, an African American friend who lived around the corner from me. Overhearing fragments of a conversation between my parents and some neighbors about Dr. King's death, I could not make sense of the violence that ended his life. I have made many efforts in the intervening years trying to make sense of racial realities in this country. I have approached this so imperfectly as a privileged, white male, but I have attempted it. I cannot know what the attempts to make sense of racial realities in the United States have been like for African Americans. I've listened intently and tried to learn and understand as much as I can, but I cannot know that experience. What I do know is that the struggle is far from over.

It's not that we haven't made progress at times, but we continue to encounter reversals, detours, reinterpretations, and delays. We should not be experiencing the revival of deadly prejudices all these years later, but here we are. Four hundred years after the first enslaved people were brought to these shores, over two hundred and twenty-five years after our nation's founding, and over a hundred and fifty years since the Emancipation Proclamation, we still fall tragically short of liberty and justice for all.

Articles, reports, and stories can easily be found, but they often do not register. I'll offer three examples of situations that cry out for attention, compassion, and justice here, but hundreds of these can be cited, including some, I bet, in your own community.

- In an article aptly entitled "Injustice on Repeat," Michelle Alexander argues that the United States remains in deep denial about systemic racism, noting the twin tragedies of mass incarceration and mass deportation.[1]

- Former South Carolina governor Nikki Haley has migrated among different positions on the Confederate flag. She first supported its presence at the Statehouse as a symbol of Southern heritage, but then boldly ordered it removed after a white supremacist murdered nine African American churchgoers in Charleston in 2015. More recently, though, she has said that the murderer made the flag stand for something other than what it meant in the first place. Many would argue that Dylan Roof made that flag stand for exactly its original message.[2]

- In another episode of reinterpretation, the acting director of US Citizenship and Immigration Services, Ken Cuccinelli, argued that the poem by Emma Lazarus did not intend to welcome everybody regardless of where they might come from on the globe, but instead to apply only to Europeans. Cuccinelli later attempted some context for his remarks, but his additional comments only inflamed the issue.[3]

## Why This Issue Matters

Human dignity and safety are the obvious reasons this matters first. We may not pay the price of it immediately, but we diminish

1. Alexander, "Injustice on Repeat."
2. Behrmann, "Nikki Haley."
3. Morin, "Immigration Official Ken Cuccinelli."

ourselves when we diminish each other. When we allow systems to remain in place that work on our behalf to diminish others, we excuse ourselves from accountability and concern. This issue also matters because it reveals the character of our country.

After a season of some optimism and modest progress, we now realize that a terrible setback has occurred. Voter rights won in the 1960s through sacrifice, injury, and death get reversed through voter suppression and gerrymandering fifty years later. Freedom secured through marches and protests by one generation disappear within two generations' time through the world's most extensive mass incarceration of nonviolent offenders in the world.

These are only two examples of fairly recent reversals, but it's not a new endeavor. Even if Reconstruction following the Civil War had put in place fair policies and accessible resources, which it failed miserably to do, groups like the United Daughters of the Confederacy would still have not rested until they rewrote the narrative about the cause and outcome of the Civil War. Reversals do not present a new phenomenon. Those leading this reversal seem determined to shape a future where white supremacy and nationalism gain control and do not let go of it.

We are experiencing what Van Jones terms "whitelash," the highly charged, negative response on the part of some white people to progress in the United States on racial equality and to the success of African Americans. Whitelash fueled the efforts to rewrite the narrative following the Civil War and to undermine Reconstruction. Pent up whitelash energies from the Obama presidency found an open channel and seemingly a blessing during the Trump campaign and presidency through explicit comments and by not immediately disavowing racist groups that supported his candidacy. The rhetoric of white supremacy has moved from a fringe element to the mainstream. A friend said to me, "If you don't have kids of color, it's hard to understand how Trump sounds."

But don't take my word for it. The Division of Homeland Security added white supremacist violence to its list of priority threats in September 2019. White Supremacists perpetrated thirty-nine of fifty domestic extremism–related murders in 2018, while jihadists were linked to only one. In a speech at the Brookings Institute, acting DHS secretary Kevin McAleenan said, "The continuing menace of racially based violent extremism, particularly white supremacist extremism, is an abhorrent affront to our nation, the struggle and unity of its diverse population, and the core values of both our society and our department." This isn't a liberal preacher or a left-wing group throwing this idea out to see if gains any traction. No, this is the federal government saying that white supremacist violence is a real problem that must be acknowledged and addressed.

Racial tensions continue to accelerate, but they are not limited to the tension between African Americans and Eurocentric Americans. A young man, enraged by anti-immigrant venom, drove 650 miles to El Paso to massacre twenty-two people at a Walmart. Threats hover over the rights and protections LGBTQ persons gained in recent years. Strident, hate-fueled, policy-enabled discrimination results every day in violence against trans persons. And just when things seem to settle a little, at least long enough to attempt dialogue and collaboration, another white police officer kills an African American woman, man, or child.

The resurgence we have seen of white supremacy and racial violence did not come about because white people like me suddenly thought less of African Americans. Its revival occurred because of our silence, our looking away while others plotted, our lack of engagement with our political system, and our tragically silly belief that simply thinking fondly of African Americans, LatinX neighbors, LGTBQ friends and others is enough.

## The Witness of the Church

The church cannot solve the scourge of racism, but neither can we continue to be complicit in it.

God's vision for the world makes no room for the demeaning of any of our sisters and brothers or any exclusion based on skin pigmentation, sexual identity or orientation, or place of origin. There are no indispensable individuals or communities. We are all God's beloved. God shows no partiality[4] and tells us to see each other not from our limited, incomplete point of view, but as the new creation of God that we are.[5] The church is the community where "there is no longer Jew or Greek, there is no longer slave or free, there is no longer male and female; for all are one in Christ Jesus."[6] We are called to treat one another as beloved, but make no mistake, the powers and principalities[7] often lash out at generous spirits, inclusive policies, and caring equanimity. Somebody is benefitting when the system turns in the direction of hate, exclusion, and violence. Otherwise, the system would not turn in that direction.

A faith infused and energized by God's vision for the world makes no room for the discrimination and danger with which too many people live. This means more than not harming someone with words or weapons. It calls for our religious, social, economic, and political involvement. Our holy thoughts and our justice-focused work are for the sake of the well-being of all people and, trust me, threatened and persecuted people are waiting and wondering who will speak and act on their behalf. And yet, so few conversations about human dignity and racial equality find their footing, sustain momentum, and lead to actions that effect constructive, fair and compassionate change.

Dr. King asked in a sermon delivered in 1967 at New York's Riverside Church, "Is our country planning on building on political myth again and then shoring it up with new violence?" I hope not, but attempts are being made in palaces of power and out-of-the-way locales to shift the narrative to renew deadly prejudices, to make room for those prejudices in the public square, to embolden dangerous impulses, and to enact new forms of discrimination that we may have considered long since extinguished. You may not be encountering this directly or daily, but many are.

Sure, some examples of progress can be lifted up. Montgomery, Alabama, elected its first black mayor. In that same state, a

4. Acts 10:34.

5. 2 Cor 5:16–17.

6. Gal 3:28.

7. Eph 6:12.

candidate who spewed ignorance and vitriol toward African Americans was denied in his bid for the US Senate. Multiracial and multicultural congregations can be found here and there as signs that some are still motivated by the vision of the beloved community. Sandhya Jha, a Disciples of Christ minister and community activist in Oakland, provides examples of many religious organizations that are attempting to confront and eliminate patterns of hate violence before the violence occurs.[8] As I'll share in a later letter, some communities and schools have committed to reparations for the lasting harm of slavery. Groups regularly go to the US-Mexico border to gain firsthand understanding of what is happening there so that they, in turn, can be advocates for a humane immigration practice and a fair immigration policy. And more and more congregations and denominations are participating in anti-racism/pro-reconciliation training.

It's time to bury deadly prejudices, not revive them. It's time to disrupt a system that works for a few and develop one that works for the many. It's past time, and tragically so.

In trust that we shall overcome,
Bill

## Questions for Discussion

1. What is so core to your faith that it leads you to actively resist the revival of deadly prejudices in this country?

2. To what examples can you point that show racism and white supremacy gaining renewed strength?

3. How will your belief in the equality and dignity of all people shape the votes you will cast for various races in the 2020 US election?

8. See Jha, *Transforming Communities*.

# 7

# Unresolved Grief and the Tenderness Deficit

My Sisters and Brothers,

I BELIEVE WE ARE a grieving nation. We are an innovating, discovering, giving, building, and worshipping nation, but we also are a grieving one. Our losses—the actual ones, the perceived ones, and the anticipated ones—have caused a palpable grief to swell within and among us, leaving us to work through uncertainty, to question our worth, to scramble to address immediate needs, and to wonder what the future holds.

We all have experienced a loss of some kind—a person we loved, a relationship, a job, a way of life, a belief we once thought unshakeable, an innocence toward the world. The wonders of technology have altered manufacturing forever. New jobs may come to the Rust Belt, but fewer and fewer of the old ones will return. Miners know the coal industry is erratic. It's been that way for over a century. Only within recent years have elected leaders attempted to turn the fluctuating coal demand into a wedge issue.

We grieve over lives lost to gun violence while elected leaders sit by and watch, beholden to special interest groups with deep pockets and fanatic followers. We grieve the attacks made on

LGBTQ persons, rhetorically and physically. We grieve the suffering at the US/Mexican border. We grieve the farm families whose
losses have mounted to the point that selling their land to an agri-
business giant seems like the only option. We grieve the policies
and appointments that have worked intentionally to exclude diverse voices and undermine understanding among diverse peoples. We grieve that the character of our nation continues to erode
with public pronouncements that assault whole groups of people
and insult the rest of us with their meanness and shortsightedness.

We know more change is on the way, a change that will cause
a good number of people tremendous consternation and grief. Our
country's population will become "minority white" in less than
twenty-five years.[1] The burgeoning youthful diversity may lead
the United States into a new era of mutuality and collaboration,
but many will find this new reality hard to swallow. As recently as
1960, whites constituted 89 percent of the US population.[2]

Candidate Trump said, "We're going to win so much. You're
going to get tired of winning. You're going to say, 'Please Mr. President, I have a headache. Please, don't win so much. This is getting
terrible.' And I'm going to say, 'No, we have to make America great
again.' You're gonna say, 'Please.' I said, 'Nope, nope. We're gonna
keep winning.'"[3]

That announcement caused some of the grieving to lift their
heads in hope. Somebody, they believed, finally recognized their
plight, understood their losses, and pledged to make it right again.
Somebody finally remembered them, brought them back into the
American family, and promised to fight the liberal locust on their
behalf. At the same time, another part of the country fell into deep
grief as it watched the Obamas leave the White House. President
Obama's departure would have been difficult on its own for many
people, but to see his successor begin immediately to dismantle
and reverse signature accomplishments made it almost unbearable.

---

1. Frey, "U.S. Will Become 'Minority White' in 2045."
2. United States Census, 1960.
3. Trump, "We're Going to Win So Much."

## Why This Issue Matters

Like many, we Americans do not always deal with grief in a helpful way. Grief emerges as a powerful emotion unlike any other in its ability to strip away the veneer of our lives. It leaves us unsure what we can count on and where we can look for safety and security.

At the first hint of such unwelcome and unsettling news, we look for someone to blame. And then, our apocalyptic impulses kick into high gear and we start looking for a savior. In a country as broad and richly diverse as ours, we hope and look for different things in a savior. We especially warm to a savior who shares our anger and who will call out, preferably in nasty terms, those who are to blame for the totally unnecessary losses. The savior promises something for everyone, regardless of political party or whether those things are affordable or wise or possible, and then predicts that we will soon know victory again. In the book of Joel, that promise came in these words: "I will repay you for the years that the swarming locust has eaten."[4] In the United States, it took the form of a slogan: "Make America Great Again."

Grief that goes unnamed, unaddressed, and unresolved turns into other things, like depression, anger, conflict, and violence. I do not think that our future can be as bright as we want it to be until we are honest about our losses and we learn to live with each other in those losses in a more constructive way than we have so far.

We attempt to deny our losses and refute our finitude. It's in our DNA as a country. Our manifest destiny, American exceptionalism and standing in the world do not prepare a people to deal with loss and change. We Americans have told each other and the world, almost from the start, that the limits and constraints that other countries face do not apply to us. We expand horizons and generate possibilities when it appears that no further expansion is possible. We hold to a national narrative that says our country does not decline, ever. And we do not respond kindly to news that our resources are limited and that our days are numbered.

4. Joel 2:25.

We Americans especially resist being told that, like the rest of humanity, we carry all the marks of finitude. We go to great lengths to deny the earth-shattering news that, as Joshua put it, we too will "go the way of all the earth."[5]

## The Witness of the Church

Scripture not only names the reality of loss and describes the accompanying grief in various places, it also tells us how we can approach one another in grief and begin to rebuild.

Do you remember the words that begin Isaiah 40? "Comfort, O comfort my people, says your God. Speak tenderly to Jerusalem." Thankfully, we are not in the condition Jerusalem was six hundred years before Jesus was born. The city lay in ruins after being been overrun by the Babylonians. Grief had set in.

We've been there. How will we deal with this diagnosis, we ask? How will we deal with this family conflict, this community violence, this economic downturn, this political crisis, this social upheaval, this threat of war? Even with the differences, though, the passage offers something to all who are looking for a way to move through grief together and reclaim the best of their lives.

The question before God and the heavenly council in Isaiah 40 was, "How will we deal with a grieving people?" And the word came simply, "Speak tenderly to Jerusalem."

Speak tenderly. It's not a time for bluster and bombast. People are hurting. Uncertainty fills much of our world. We are fragile and vulnerable. It's no time for name-calling and provocation. It's no time to let our insecurities dictate our words and direct our actions.

Let tenderness register first. Start with a tender word. Speak tenderly to Jerusalem. And speak tenderly to El Paso and Ferguson and Parkland. Speak tenderly where factories are shuttered and fields are no longer farmed. Speak tenderly to Baja and Sonora, to Syria and Palestine, to urban cores and rural crossroads, and to all those places where grief grips God's beloved children.

---

5. Jer 23:14.

Speak tenderly into the pain of communities under siege. Speak tenderly when people are navigating unimaginable change. Speak tenderly to the searching soul, to the child in our midst, to the aging parent, to the repeat offender frustrated with herself, to the wayward son unsure if coming home is an option, to the determined enemy, to the estranged friend, to the person across our breakfast table, to the one in the pew beside us, in front of us, behind us. Speak tenderly.

British actor Alan Rickman said, "If only life could be a little more tender, and art more robust." We have a tenderness deficit in our world and it is never more apparent than when we are raw from loss and spinning from change. That's what Rickman was pointing to. It's present in our own country and too often in our own churches and even sometimes in our own families. We've got the bluster down, the shock and awe, the threats, the sheer power, the might, the exaggerated rhetoric, the egotistical pronouncements, the barrage of innuendo and false trails.

We cannot and will not out-bluster some people, but I am not sure we are quite ready to trust tenderness. We aren't convinced that speaking tenderly is effective speech or a plausible approach. To be tender is to be weak in the eyes of many, to give up too much ground at the start, to dismiss that genuine vulnerability has any place in our public discourse and our personal relationships. What is truer is that it takes enormous calm, strength, and courage to speak tenderly in the face of wreckage and hostility.

We are the answers to the tenderness deficit. Our presence, our words, our actions—we are the answers to the tenderness deficit. We show forth the pure, unbounded Love that is at the center of the universe. We speak hope into the hurting places of people's lives with a tender word of healing, of justice, and of hope. We participate in the tender uplift of grieving people, not the beating down of those ready to give up.

I understand why people don't trust tenderness. Some days, it just doesn't sound much like a viable strategy for when times are hard. And it cannot be the only strategy, not every day and not in every situation.

But we think God must trust tenderness. It's right there in Isaiah at one of the most critical times in Israel's history. God speaks tenderly to Jerusalem to provide a way for the people. With all the loss and destruction, the people might not have otherwise heard God's voice. Even more, with all the rebuilding ahead and with the living in new circumstances with new neighbors, God wanted Israel to learn the pitch and tone of tenderness so that they in turn would learn to trust it for their living in the world.

I know it seems questionable, at best, but think about it. When God set out again to provide a way for us, God chose the most tender of all ways to come among us. God apparently believes that one way to turn the world back toward its loving, hopeful, just direction is through tenderness. God apparently believes that one way to topple oppression and reverse regimes is by way of tenderness.

And out of that divine belief God now says to you and me, "Speak tenderly to the Jerusalems of your lives and to the grief of your neighbors and comfort, o comfort, my people."

Tenderly,
Bill


## Questions for Discussion

1. What grief lingers with you as a result of changes in your life, in your church, in your community, and in our country and how do you deal with it?

2. In what ways do you find comfort and hope in your life of faith and through the church?

3. In what ways will changes and losses, both those felt already and the anticipated ones, shape your thinking and participation in the 2020 US election?

# 8

# A Desire to Be Hopeful and Helpful

My Sisters and Brothers,

I AM AMAZED AND inspired by the incredible things that individuals and organizations are doing to ease suffering and address unjust systems. So much good is happening. The righteous tenacity of these individuals and organizations focuses and fuels their efforts, even though it almost always is scrappy work and very often undertaken with modest resources. Some of the most amazing people do this work, week after week, year after year. When they love their neighbors, they do more than think warmly of them from time to time. They come alongside their neighbors to affirm their humanity, gifts, and wisdom, even as the neighbors weather daily the harsh conditions of the margins.

In some cases, the efforts address the circumstances of a particular season and attempt to ease the suffering of a particularly difficult stretch. In other cases, individuals and organizations identify the multiple systems that are running in the background of, for example, a community mired in intergenerational poverty and together work on the root causes of the situation, such as safety, housing, transportation, education, food access, and reentry to the community following incarceration. One person or group cannot address all the angles and systems that keep people in poverty, but we all can be involved in one of these areas and, together, we can address the systemic causes.

Are you aware of the efforts that are occurring in your town or city or region? I thought of myself as being fairly familiar with the efforts in Indianapolis where I live. I often have found myself describing the positive impact of an organization to people who were unaware of it, but I realize I only know of some of the efforts. It seems that every few weeks I learn of another effort in the community.

People want to be hopeful and helpful and that desire is taking on concrete expression in hurting lives and struggling communities. So that it might cause you to look around and take note of the good that is happening near you, I'll share a few examples with which I am acquainted.

- You Yes You connects daughters with their incarcerated dads through events in correctional facilities. A much better chance exists for an ongoing relationship with daughters once the dads are released from prison if that relationship can be kept intact or renewed while the dads are still incarcerated. Those occasions, which are usually dances for the dads and daughters, must involve significant awkwardness and navigating enormous bureaucratic tape, but Ericka, the founder of You Yes You in Indianapolis, knows that her organization's efforts are changing lives through rebuilding and maintaining these relationships. The daughters and the dads will have a different future as a result.

- Brianna's Hope emerged out of tragedy. The young woman, who spent nearly half of her twenty-five-year life battling drug abuse, was found dead near the small town of Red Key, Indiana, in 2014 after going missing for ten weeks. The opioid epidemic had claimed another life as it swept without discrimination across much of the Midwest. Rev. Randy Davis, a United Methodist pastor, knew that Brianna was just one of many in Red Key and towns like it who were struggling with addiction, so he began Brianna's Hope. "I convinced myself that a sloppy start was better than no start," Davis told one of my classes at Christian Theological Seminary. I'm not sure it was a sloppy start, but it was a modest one. Now, from one tragedy in a small town and a pastor who had never undertaken anything like this before, Brianna's Hope has grown to thirty-six chapters in two states, all because someone who knew that this could not stand decided to do something about it.

• Faith in Indiana, a local chapter of a national community organizing network, works on a grassroots, nonpartisan, interfaith basis to effect change in local systems. The faith communities who are part of this organization have little in common in many instances, but their heart for the well-being of the city bring them together for direct action on issues like public transportation, gun violence reduction, immigration, diversity training for public servants, and voter engagement. One person told me, "I would never have thought five years ago that I would be making cold calls and walking neighborhoods to raise awareness of the issues and to encourage people to vote, but I realized that the city and state weren't going to act for good without some pressure from people like me."

## Why This Issue Matters

I offer the examples above just to point you toward similar efforts in your areas of the country. A couple of notes should accompany these examples. First, not only are diverse groups of people coming together for healing and uplift, but I promise you that some of the people you least like are working to improve the quality of life for us all. Senator Mitch McConnell and Speaker Nancy Pelosi represent the vast difference in perspectives and priorities among our elected leaders at every level. Not only have those two led legislation for the benefit of hurting people and struggling communities, the people we associate with their views on local and state levels likely have generated some positive outcomes. It's not been enough yet and the gridlock and vitriol are despicable, but in my most honest moments I admit that I am aware that people I often find offensive are not without some merit.

Second, we usually will not become acquainted with the good that is happening around us, much less become involved with it, if we are glued to our favorite echo chamber–like news source. The good news will get drowned out by commentators whose job security depends on an audience deeply entangled in anxiety and fear, an audience that refuses to entertain the possibility that progress is being made on some important situations and issues. It falls to us to know our community and both its strengths and its challenges better. People everywhere are taking that first step and then becoming involved. It's really rather remarkable. Despite what you might think from what can seem like an enveloping despair, many of us remain hopeful and helpful. That's a beautiful expression of both the American spirit and the Christian vocation.

As Americans, we usually come together following the hurricane, the shooting, and the fatal train or plane crash. It's what we do and in those moments we have exhibited an uplifting goodwill, even if at times we quickly squandered that goodwill. These days, however, we struggle to move beyond political attacks even in the midst of national concerns and tragedies. We see an opportunity in the midst of great pain to leverage our position or our party and we seize it.

That's why it is so important to lift up and keep before us these remarkable efforts that are going on all around us. Many of them are bearing noticeable, measurable fruit. Men and women are re-entering communities following incarceration more prepared to lead lives of peace and purpose. Families are taking advantage of housing options that only a few years ago were not available or affordable. Churches are focusing on building up the community of a single zip code through a variety of services and resources. Communities are partnering with groups of all kinds to create and sustain neighborhoods where life can be known again and enjoyed. If you desire to be hopeful and helpful, you are far from alone as a great array of individuals and organizations exercise their hopefulness and helpfulness in creative ways.

## The Witness of the Church

So what does an example of this hopefulness and helplessness look like in and through the church? Again, many examples and stories illustrate good efforts. One of my favorites is from the Presbyterian Church (U.S.A.), which in the summer of 2019 called the Rev. Deanna Hollas to be this country's first known Minister of Gun Violence Prevention. Rev. Hollas grew up in Plainview, Texas, where guns and hunting are part of the culture. She will continue to serve in her ministry in Richardson, Texas, along with this newly created denominational post. She decries the tens of thousands of Americans who are killed or injured every year in senseless and unrestrained acts of gun violence. Saying that we need to do more than react to the latest mass shooting, Rev. Hollas will focus on providing education, encouragement, and care to congregations and communities across the country who seek to eliminate gun violence.

Like community leaders and organizations described earlier in this letter whose hopefulness and helpfulness are taking on concrete expression and leading to positive impact, the Presbyterian Peace Fellowship's action to designate a Minister of Gun Violence Prevention elevates the urgency of this issue and signals a clear commitment on the part of the church.

In Deuteronomy 30 the word comes to the Israelites: "I have set before you life and death, blessings and curses. Choose life so that you and your descendants may live."[1] Our choosing of life is not a single choice made in the abstract, but choosing life over and over again in the face of specific issues and contexts. The ministry of Rev. Hollas represents that choosing and calls to us to make our own choices for life, even and especially when the better resourced, better connected work day and night against us.

At the installation service for Rev. Hollas, which was held at Westminster Presbyterian Church in Dallas, the gathered sang a hymn written by Carolyn Winfrey Gillette following the 2017 church shooting in Sutherland Springs, Texas. As important as

---

1. Deut 30:19.

thoughts and prayers are, the hymn speaks to hopefulness and helpfulness taking on concrete expression. The hymn, to the tune of O WALY WALY, is entitled "If We Just Talk of Thoughts and Prayers."[2]

> If we just talk of thoughts and prayers
> And don't live out a faith that dares,
> And don't take on the ways of death,
> Our thoughts and prayers are fleeting breath.
> If we just dream of what could be
> And do not build community,
> And do not seek to change our ways,
> Our dreams of change are false displays.
> If we just sing of doing good
> And don't walk through our neighborhood
> To learn its hope, to ease its pain,
> Our talk of good is simply vain.
> God, may our prayers and dreams and songs
> Lead to a faith that takes on wrongs—
> That works for peace and justice, too.
> Then will our prayers bring joy to you.

It's worth saying again—I am amazed and inspired by what individuals and organizations are doing in our communities. The work is particularly moving in a time when hopefulness gets beaten down and helpfulness gets criticized. Even if others want to drag us down, we seek to be hopeful. Even if those who hold power and purse cannot and will not support us, we will work to be helpful.

Giving thanks for all the hopeful, helpful people,
Bill

---

2. Gillette, "If We Just Talk."

## Questions for Discussion

1. If you could change one specific situation in our country right now, what would it be and why?

2. Still thinking about that one specific situation, what are the first three steps you can take toward bringing about the needed change?

3. How will your desire to see this particular change occur lead you to assess the candidates and shape your involvement in the 2020 US election?

# What We Hope For

## 9

# To See Ourselves in the
# American Family Portrait

My Sisters and Brothers,

SOMETHING CHANGED ON NOVEMBER 4, 2008. Not as much changed as needed to change and some people and groups have been busy trying to undo what did change that night, but especially considering our country's history, the election of Barak Obama represented a significant development that many thought they would never see. The United States had elected an African American man as president.

We had come a long way as a country. Nearly 70 million people cast votes for Obama, which is more votes than any presidential candidate has ever received. He also won a decisive Electoral College victory, flipping numerous states that only rarely had voted Democratic in recent elections.

Along with the making of history, the 2008 election resonated on a deeply personal level. Cameras scanned the crowd at Chicago's Grant Park on election night while Obama spoke, capturing the tearful joy and palpable apprehension of some of the nation's most prominent African Americans. "Is this really happening? Has the United States of America just elected a black man as its president?" They braced for Obama to experience incredible scrutiny and for any Obama shortcoming to serve as evidence in the minds of some that African Americans do not possess the intelligence and wherewithal to govern and lead. They also worried about his safety. While he faced many demeaning remarks related to his race, President Obama completed two terms without being on the receiving end of physical violence. However, the fact that people worried to an unusual degree about this possibility indicates the depth of alienation between African American and certain Eurocentric communities.

But another personal dimension surfaced that night that some of us should recognize and never forget. Earlier that day, my wife and I had taken our two young children with us to the polling booth for what we believed would be a historic day. As I cast my vote, it occurred to me again that I did not know what it was like not to have someone who looked like me in the White House. Before President Obama, people like me were forty-three for forty-three when it came to presidential elections.[1] I have been happier on some election nights than others, but I always have been able to see my gender, race, and social location in the face of the US president.

Of course, tears flowed that night in Grant Park. For the first time ever, some people were able to see themselves represented in the one who had just been elected to the presidency. They hoped that Obama's election was a signal not only that they could expect more faces of color in the White House but that the nation had taken another step toward becoming a more inclusive community.

Eight years later, many people felt deep disappointment when Secretary Clinton did not win the 2016 election. The disappointed group includes women who longed to see for the first time something of themselves in the person of the president. At the same time, when Donald Trump won the 2016 presidential election, many saw the president-elect as one who spoke on behalf of forgotten people from large swaths of the country. Trump's populist

---

1. Barak Obama is the forty-fourth president of the United States. The 2008 election was the fifty-sixth US presidential election. Several elections led to the reelection of a sitting president.

strategies and antiestablishment rhetoric caught the attention of people, especially in the South and along the Rust Belt, who for a long time had felt abandoned and excluded from the American family photo. Most of those folks have little in common with Donald Trump, but they believed he would act on their behalf and look out for their concerns in ways that no one had in a long time. Whether a sufficient number of them believe that has proven to be the case will be at the heart of the 2020 election.

## Why This Issue Matters

President Lincoln concluded his famous Gettysburg Address by longing for a "new birth of freedom," one that promises a government "of the people, by the people, for the people."[2] Unfortunately, our country has struggled and continues to struggle with what we mean by "the people" in those closing words of Lincoln's speech. The term "the people" rarely means all of the people, even though we have no greater treasure in this country than our people, in all our beautiful diversity and complementary perspectives. We may wish that it means all of us. We may even get caught up in a patriotic frenzy and make claims that it means all of us, but crafty leaders over time have set us against each other in fierce competition, usually as a diversion so that we won't notice that large corporations and ideological special interests are setting the agenda instead of "the people."

We all want and deserve to see ourselves represented in the articulation of American values and, at least to some extent, in the body of elected officials. We all want and deserve to have our background, perspective, and hope recognized and taken into consideration in public discourse and policy. We all want and deserve to be able to hear the best parts of our national narrative and say, "That's my story, that's my story!"

Even though many will not see themselves represented in the face and life of a US president, we can expect and even demand

2. Lincoln, *Great Speeches*, 104.

that every US president hold all people in dignity, look out for the concerns of all people, and call all of us to a shared life of flourishing. I hear and read the meanness that groups visit upon each other. Our leaders should not be able to participate and stoke blatant cruelty like that without consequences. Situations will surface frequently where the age-old challenge of doing the most good for the most people will represent a very steep challenge. At that point, let us hear the call to discern and imagine together rather than letting that time become a humiliation fest of demeaning each other, dismissing each other's concerns, and intentionally dividing us against each other. We have a long history in this country of people from all parts and parties participating in that kind of belittling speech and derisive action. It has led to a moment when little interest or motivation exists to come back together in common cause.

Think about our country as a large, beautiful family photo. Think about the hopes and dreams represented in that photo, as well as the motivations behind such a stunning array of Americans. The person who wins the 2020 presidential election will have a lot to say about who gets to be in the American family picture, who gets to stay in that photo, and whether everyone gets treated fairly and supportively. The 2020 election is really about the character and basic commitments of our country. The irony that emerging facial recognition software may threaten and keep out those who otherwise would be in the American family photo angers me greatly.

Just "breathing free," as the poem on the Statue of Liberty describes it, is a start, but only a start. The next step is for people to trust that they are safe and secure. Still another step is for people to know affirmation and appreciation. All that has to happen in order for us to feel included in the grand photo and in the articulation of American values.

## The Witness of the Church

A few years ago my church tradition and several others began using the slogan "All Means All." You may think that was an unnecessary announcement. After all, isn't that like "rain means rain" or "football means football?" We usually don't speak one word and then, in order to clarify it, repeat that same word as its definition, unless of course some history exists that calls into question whether we have really meant what we have said when we have spoken that word.

When it comes to the church, too often all has not meant all. People have responded to the announcement that "All Are Welcome" on a neighborhood church sign only to find out that isn't the case. Scripture often speaks of "all," calling *all* who are weary and carrying heavy burdens to a house of prayer for *all* peoples,[3] but too often *all* meant white people or straight people or property owners or the socialites of a community. And when it came to leadership, *all* meant even fewer of us.

In other words, the church's embrace and inclusion sometimes suffers from the same misrepresentation that our country exhibits. This calls for acts of confession, hope, and healing, which I will discuss in letter 15, but it also gives us the opportunity to continue to consider our vocation. Here are two examples of how the church's voice can work to make a place in the family portrait for those who seek to be included and recognized.

First, much of the world is experiencing a massive refugee crisis right now. An estimated 30 million people are seeking safety and a fresh start because of persecution, violence and dire economic circumstances in their homeland. In the early 1980s, the United States accepted 200,000 refugees annually. We received an average of 67,000 newcomers during the Obama administration. For 2020, that number will be 18,000. Those trying to cross into the United States from Mexico are enduring brutal conditions and unnecessarily long detentions.

As the church, we can begin by trying to transform hostility and prejudice into hospitality and acceptance, but opportunities

---

3. Matt 11:28 and Isa 56:7.

for our influence also exist on the systemic scale. As people of faith, we have a responsibility to address policy makers, both at election time and in between elections, on behalf of those whose lives continue to be at risk. A starting point would be for the country to come clean on what drives our policies. Some cite a lack of resources. Others fear large-scale drug trafficking. But in the end, is this really about the efforts of some to ensure that certain groups do not show up in the American family portrait? It's hard for me to wrap my mind around the rhetoric and the brutality otherwise.

Second, the White Nationalist movement continues to gain traction as it seeks to bring into the mainstream an argument that existed only on the fringes until recently. The threat of nationalism emerges most gravely when people begin by promoting the prominence and power of their country, but then quickly couple their nationalistic impulses with a stunningly narrow view of who truly represents the country's rightful heirs and powerbrokers. If Stephen Miller is influenced by the company he keeps with white nationalists and then peddles that influence as an advisor to President Trump, it's no wonder that issues like revoking birthright citizenship and ending DACA continue to be actions that the administration, as President Trump phrased it, is looking at "very, very seriously."

Until the church and others with a passion for justice speak, act, vote, and protest against such moves, that is, until the church proclaims in one, loud, compelling voice the dignity of every human being, the regression and division will continue and worsen. Discouraging stories and demeaning policies will continue to inform and influence the ethos of our country.

The 2020 presidential election is not the only occasion or referendum on some of these polices, but it is a very important one.

For an American family photo that includes everybody,
Bill

## Questions for Discussion

1. What issue of inclusion and diversity either in the church or broader community has challenged you the most and why?

2. Many of us recited the pledge of allegiance beginning in the early years of elementary school. What are three ways for you to become involved in advocating for those people who remain outside the pledge's vision of "with liberty and justice for all"?

3. Of the many issues being debated during the 2020 US election season, how important are proposed policies related to immigration as you consider candidates for whom to vote?

*10*

# To Know and Trust
# One Another Again

My Sisters and Brothers,

ONE IMAGE IN PARTICULAR disturbed a lot of Americans in 2019. I'm not referring to pictures of the Antarctic ice sheet melting at an accelerating rate, or caged children at the Mexican border, or Greta Thunberg speaking at the United Nations, or President Trump standing alongside Kim Jong Un, though none of those went unnoticed and, in some cases, sparked various responses and emotions. I am referring to something else. It happened in Texas. At a football game. In a private luxury box. And many in the country viewed it as scandalous.

For about four hours on October 6, 2019, former President George W. Bush and Ellen DeGeneres sat, talked, and laughed together at a Dallas Cowboys football game. Imagine the gall these two possess that they would not honor the political lines that many have drawn. And not only did Bush and DeGeneres collapse the opposing categories established in this country, they looked like they were having a good time doing it. How dare those two act as if anybody in this country can be friends!

I admit that there are people I would not go to a football game with, but if we can return to the real world for just a minute. Imagine how divided a country must be and how utterly suspicious we are toward each other if we take this level of offense at two people enjoying a football game together. Social media lit up for days. Ellen did not take well to the Twitter-shaming attempted by those who accused her of betrayal and careless judgment. George W. Bush offered his own defense of his friendship with Ellen. What I interpreted as an unusually encouraging sign enraged groups at nearly all points on the political spectrum. Meanwhile, back at the US-Mexico border and at Pyongyang and on the dwindling polar icecap, too many were digging their heels into positions from which little progress on real issues is likely.

We sometimes confuse the experience of *knowing of* people with the experience of actually *knowing* people. We can know of someone and incur very little risk and vulnerability. "Knowing of" can happen at physical and emotional distance. We might use "knowing of" as a way to absolve ourselves of any interrelatedness and responsibility. We can know of individuals and groups and never learn a new thing about them. We can even know of people and countries and still drop bombs on them.

It's harder to be violent toward individuals and groups when we know each other and are not just vaguely familiar with each other's existence. When we know each other, we know names, places, and ways of life that are important to all of us. When we know each other, we involve ourselves for the sake of others' well-being. The emotional distance closes. Energy and appreciation fill the physical spaces where we gather. When we know each other, trust can begin to develop. And if we are attempting to share life with each other in even the simplest of ways, trust is essential. Things break down pretty quickly when people try and occupy the same physical and emotional space in the absence of trust.

## Why This Issue Matters

Much of the country seems content simply to know of each other and sometimes barely that. In some cases, people who once knew and trusted each other have backed out of those relationships, often over a single candidate, a very narrow set of issues, or their own political or financial aspirations. The environment often feels like the hyped-up posture taken between sports rivals, management and labor negotiations, legal disputes, and international conflicts. In all these cases, having an enemy helps keep our fighting edge and, as some dreadfully put it, our killer instinct.

The less we know each other the more latitude we take in how we think of each other, talk about each other, and act toward each other. That is especially the case these days now that past norms of restraint and decorum no longer apply for many. Urban dwellers and those in small towns and rural areas know of each other at best. The same can be said of people in much of the Northeast and many in the Deep South. Exceptions exist, thankfully, but for the most part they only know of each other. Political leaders and media outlets encourage that kind of emotional distance. The geographical distance simply confirms it.

Pro-life and pro-choice people know of each other. Rarely would people from one of those camps trust people from the other camp to even hear their story, much less to be brought face to face in a time of vulnerable sharing and partnership. Fierce protectors of the Second Amendment and groups who work for sensible gun reforms may know of each other, but that conversation has so completely jumped the tracks of integrity and reason that they may not even admit to that much right now.

I not only wonder how long this kind of toxic distance can go on, I also wonder how long those who stoke and preserve this animus toward each other can go on before our country either deteriorates beyond recognition and recovery or does something about it. And yet, just as we can think of people with whom we would never share any tender part of our story because it would be unsafe and unwise, we find ourselves in a very similar position in this country. We will not "elect" our way out of this. That is, we will not be able to steady and focus the country's wildly swinging pendulum only by looking to the next election cycle. At some point, we will have to relearn and recommit to talking and working with each other.

Whether we are talking about the United States Congress or a town council, someone has to act from a presumption of good faith to even give problem-solving and collaboration a chance. Whether we are debating immigration or Affirmative Action, any movement forward will only occur, as Stephen Covey phrased it, at the speed of trust, which is the speed of moving from knowing of each other to knowing each other.

## The Witness of the Church

Trust is the measure of whether we have made the move from knowing of someone to knowing someone. And usually, that move involves the sharing of stories. Let me illustrate with an exercise that my teaching assistant, Cassidy Hall, facilitated with a class we taught called "Pastoral Leadership across Difference and Polarization.

We asked two students, Kara and Beverly, in advance of the class meeting if they were willing to share an experience of difference and polarization and how the challenges, pain, and missed opportunities of that experience felt. They both agreed, so we described the process to them. Kara and Beverly would sit facing each other while everyone else remained in their usual seating arranged to observe and listen. Kara would go first, telling her story of difference and polarization, and Beverly would listen. When Kara finished and we had allowed some breathing space following a story that brought up many emotions, Beverly's task was to retell Kara's story *as Kara*. In other words, Beverly didn't simply share Kara's story. No, for a few minutes, Beverly became Kara, beginning her retelling of Kara's story with, "Hi, I'm Kara. I grew up in Michigan and have lived and worked in Indianapolis for many years, including a stretch of time when I had to work alongside a prejudiced, demeaning woman who tried almost daily to sabotage my career." Beverly told Kara's story in a beautiful and heartfelt way that moved not only Kara, but everybody in the class.

Then it was Beverly's turn to share an experience when she had encountered difference and polarization. The two continued to sit face-to-face and Beverly began, "Hi, I'm Beverly, and my story really centers in the church where I've held a staff position for several years without actually feeling affirmed or supported in that ministry." Kara listened intently and lovingly as Beverly told a story of joy and disappointment repeatedly playing out in her congregational setting. When Beverly finished, it was Kara's turn to tell the same story *as Beverly*. Kara began, "Hi, I'm Beverly, and I've been a ministry associate at my church for several years. I love the work I do and I feel called to do it, but I do not feel accepted for who I am or supported for the ministry I am asked to do." Kara finished telling Beverly's story and it was time for all of us to breathe again, process what we had heard and experienced, and give thanks to Kara and Beverly for their willingness to lead the class in such an honest, attentive, and reciprocal sharing.

Kara and Beverly demonstrated something that evening that too much of our country has forgotten or chooses simply to ignore. We can speak often from a distance, from the position of know-ing of, but we do not really know each other until we know each other's stories and can tell them in the company of each other. We know each other well when we listen deeply and carefully to one another, even as the emotion of the moment rises and the honesty of the sharing makes staying in the conversation very difficult. Few occasions call for or generate more trust than when we are getting to know each other. Kara and Beverly modeled that openness and support with one another as they shared painful experiences. In turn, they modeled friendship and trust as they allowed the other to give voice to their own stories. The rest of the class participated by committing to a space where risks like that can be taken.

God has given the church the ministry of reconciliation. Whether by the approach described above or any number of other ways, the opportunity exists for people of faith to exercise the ministry of reconciliation within our congregations and in the wider community. For example, Lennon Flowers and Jennifer Bailey responded to the steep identity and idealogical differences following the 2016 presidential election by creating The People's Supper. In the last four years, they have facilitated over 1,500 meals across the country, moving people from the "knowing of" column to the "knowing" column. As Christians, we believe something good happens when we eat together. Now, we just need to get each other to the table.

What might happen if we approached one another, even if tentatively at first, believing that we will find good in each other? What if before we dared to reach across one of the political or social or religious chasms I have named here we stepped back in a moment of introspection and self-confrontation? What would change if we renewed some friendships and began moving people and groups from the "know of" column into the "know" column?"

I'd say just about everything.

Looking forward to knowing you,
Bill

## Questions for Discussion

1. What gaps in our relationships or breaches of trust in the United States pose the greatest threat to our present quality of life and the future of our country?

2. How does your faith inform the concept of trust and help you navigate experiences when trust has been broken?

3. How important is trust as you consider the votes you will cast in the 2020 US election?

## 11

# To See Courageous
# Leadership Exercised

My Sisters and Brothers,

WE TALK OFTEN ABOUT leadership. We seek it for the groups and communities of which we are part. our families, places of work, schools, churches, our communities, and our country, but it is an elusive concept. We do not share a universal definition of what leadership is. Sometimes we ask for a particular kind of leadership in a given circumstance only to realize later that a different approach would have been far more helpful.

When asked questions like "Who are our leaders?" and "What do leaders do?" we may have as many opinions as there are people in the room. And when asked, "Why do we accept some people as leaders but not others?" the opinions multiply even more. Leadership turns on personality and charisma for some. For some it is about style, with some being more comfortable with a direct, compelling approach while others appreciate a more consensus-building style. For still other people, leadership means vision-casting and problem-solving. For still others, leadership hinges solely on trust and integrity.

Debates about leadership qualities, training, and certification persist even though leadership development and training is a multimillion-dollar industry. We can scarcely pick up a magazine or click on a website without coming across leadership workshops and leadership degree programs.

Sometimes, it is easier to say what leadership is not. Leadership is not self-promoting or self-serving. It is not erratic or divisive or belittling. Leadership doesn't over—or underreact. It doesn't infuse an emotional system with increased anxiety because of its own instability. Leadership does not base its decisions to disclose or withhold information on whether doing so will lead to personal benefit or political gain. Leadership does not undermine the well-being of the community it is supposed to care for and guide.

What I value about leadership may not be what you value about leadership. And in different seasons and circumstances, I have valued different things as various sets of needs and opportunities presented themselves.

I value leadership that can bring along as much of the community or organization or congregation as possible toward the goal or vision that we have discerned and adopted. My view is that people will embrace a change in the long term if they are given space and time to work through the inevitable questioning, processing, letting go, and claiming of the new thing to which God calls us.

This approach, no doubt, comes from growing up in a very democratic family and with a small-town ethos that prized democratic decision-making. My church tradition also influences me greatly. The Christian Church (Disciples of Christ) began on the American frontier, far away from what our forebears considered to be the stifling establishment and hierarchy of Northeastern politics and church structures. We take Paul's image of the body in 1 Corinthians 12 seriously, believing that eye and ear, foot and hand, and everyone else have a valued place and voice in the church. In our movement, the minister exercises representative leadership. That is, the key work of the minister is to see that all voices in the congregation are represented at the table in an atmosphere of deep, common discernment of God's purposes and how best to respond. The leader's role is make sure this conversation takes place, and to make sure that all voices—even unpopular ones—receive a hearing.

I recognize how different this approach is, especially in today's climate. I would rather work with as many people as possible toward a good end, believing that holding as much of the community together as possible through a process will strengthen the plans and enhance the outcome. This inclination sounds almost quaint in a political environment where there is no interest or effort in bringing the country together and all the energy goes into securing a fanatical base that, at best, is barely over 50 percent of the group and thus represents a very thin majority.

## Why This Issue Matters

The election of a US president is unparalleled in the world in terms of its influence, length of process, and expense. The significant increase in the number of executive decisions made by the president, a trend that largely started with George W. Bush and continued with Barak Obama and now Donald Trump, further raises the stakes when we consider our options and cast our vote for president.

In the upcoming 2020 election, I think we face a particularly daunting challenge. The pendulum's swing between Barak Obama and Donald Trump has left us with whiplash. The Obama administration issued a large number of executive orders, many of which the Trump administration has reversed. Between these policy changes and President Trump's inclination to lead by keeping people off-balance, it's understandable why we enter this election season feeling as if a lot is riding on it. Which of Obama's executive decisions will continue or be brought back? Which ones will die? Which of Trump's executive decisions will live and which will be ended? What can we count on moving forward and what kind of leadership do we desire in a president?

For example, I find those who voted Obama-Obama-Trump (2008–2012–2016) to be a fascinating and interesting group of people. It seems to me millions of people essentially voted for the massive pendulum swing that we have felt recently, but that's not at all how they describe their participation in the 2016 election. Nor is it how they describe the state of the country. For many, our country feels more settled and confident under the Trump presidency than under any presidency of recent times. Wherever we are on that spectrum of feeling hopeful or discouraged about the state of our country and its future, most of us will agree that it is a time that calls for courageous leadership.

We see various descriptors in front of the word leadership—servant leadership, innovative leadership, missional leadership, transformational leadership. We live in a time when we need courageous leadership, even though we probably won't agree on that term anymore than we agree on the meaning of the basic term of leadership.

And again, it's helpful to say what leadership is not. The contrast will be useful in thinking about courageous leadership.

Courageous leaders refuse to give in to their worst instincts. They do not traffic in lies. They do not deal in unfounded conspiracy theories. They do not create and then keep repeating their own separate set of facts that they know are not grounded in reality and truth. And they do not allow those working alongside them to peddle lies, conspiracy theories, and deliberately misleading facts. Courageous leaders refuse to be dishonest and refuse to equivocate.

Courageous leaders do not make entire blocks of voters and major parts of the country dispensable. They do not throw words around carelessly and abuse the privilege and responsibility of public voice. Courageous leaders do not bully those who disagree with them. They do not sell their soul to the highest bidder or campaign contributor. They do not wither before great opportunities and challenges. And they do not blame others for their own lack of political will.

## The Witness of the Church

A person with whom I used to teach was fond of saying that the church has been part of every movement for social change in US history. It's a true statement, but an incomplete one. The church also has vociferously opposed and violently worked against every movement for social change in US history. Yes, in pictures from the Civil Rights Era, we see the ministers and other people of faith leading marches and protests, but more churches opposed racial equality than worked for it. Yes, some church leaders were at the forefront of ensuring rights and protections for the LGBTQ community, but more churches fought those rights and protections. Some did so through blatant efforts. Others did so through their silence. Only after the matter was essentially settled did some churches and religious leaders come on board. It's a mixed record at best and hardly one that we can credibly call courageous.

So then, what does faith-informed, courageous leadership look like in a time like this? Paul draws out several key dimensions of courage as he closes his First Letter to the Corinthians: "Keep alert, stand firm in your faith, be courageous, be strong. Let all that you do be done in love."[1] Certain practices of courageous leadership emerge from those two verses.

First, courageous leaders not only do not hide things, they trust people with information, provide the fullest picture possible, and encourage people to stay alert. Paul's urging to "stay alert" echoes Jesus' words to stay awake or watchful or alert. It's a common apocalyptic theme that gets invoked frequently in Scripture.[2] It's a reminder that every possibility, situation, and dilemma has a context. Even though we may want to look away and ignore the harsher parts of what is happening around us, courage calls us to pay attention, to take note of emerging opportunities and challenges, and to consider what our faithful response and participation will be. Courageous leaders help us to do those things.

---

1. 1 Cor 16:13–14.
2. Matt 24:42 is one example.

Second, Paul tells the Corinthians to stand firm in their faith. Courageous leaders keep our commitments, values, and priorities ever before us. That's why preaching and teaching are so critical in building up the body of Christ. We not only find trivial drivel amusing, on some level I think we like it because it allows us to ignore or least postpone things like loving our enemy, doing justice, making peace, and effecting reconciliation. Courageous leaders work constantly and hopefully to help us be shaped continually in our own story and in the church's mission. They call forth and equip other leaders to celebrate the gifts of everyone and to ensure all are sufficiently empowered and supported.

Third, Paul connects courage with strength. It takes strength to cultivate a nonreactive, emotional container that allows us to feel the urgency of an opportunity or challenge without being overwhelmed by it. Courageous leaders know the importance of providing that kind of supportive and calm atmosphere. They also know that they must set aside whatever time is necessary for their own renewal and recovery so that they can continue to nurture that kind of environment. Leaders model well-being for us and emotionally self-regulate even when the system has descended into chaos.

And finally, Paul says to let everything we do be done in love. Whatever discerning must occur, whatever difficult word must be spoken, whatever strategy is stretching us, whatever immovable mountain is before us, whatever valley we're coming up out of, courageous leaders lead by love and call others to do the same. In doing so, there is no substitute for personal authenticity, integrity, and stability.

This is one way that Scripture talks about courageous leadership. It offers lessons for civic and religious leaders alike. These are essential qualities and practices for anyone who wishes to be counted among the courageous leaders of our time.

In prayer with you for the rise of courage,
Bill

## Questions for Discussion

1. What examples of courage are presently on display in the United States?

2. What examples of cowardice are presently on display in the United States?

3. How much will you consider the importance of courage as you participate in the 2020 US election?

*12*

# To Observe and Participate in Honest Debate and Real Conversations

My Sisters and Brothers,

BRENÉ BROWN TELLS THE story of consulting with the retail giant Costco. One day before she was to speak, CEO Craig Jelinke was sharing news with Costco's senior leaders and then responding to their questions. As Brown describes it, the senior leaders were asking tough questions, the kind that often lead to a president or CEO or pastor to zig and zag without ever really acknowledging the question, much less answering it, but Jelinke's answers were equally difficult. He was delivering unwelcome news. His responses included, "Yes, we did make that decision and here's why . . .» Another response went something like, "No, we're not going in that direction and here's how we got to that decision . . .»

When Jelinke finished, the large group of senior leaders leapt to their feet in applause. Stunned and speechless, Brown said to the person sitting next to her, "That was really hard. He did not give them the answers they were looking for. Why is everyone cheering?"

And the woman replied, "Because at Costco, we clap for the truth."

I think we should clap every time public discourse, legislative debates, and executive pronouncements pursue truth through honest debate and real conversations. Wouldn't it be great if we broke into applause several times a day? It's possible, but at least these four things stand in the way for now.

First, we are lacking in trustworthy information. Debate in our country these days can be characterized, at best, as uninformed. We can attribute part of that dilemma to the complexity and range of issues, but in some cases people intentionally ignore key facts when an issue is under consideration. In other words, sometimes it is a lack of knowledge and awareness of what is at stake, but just as often candidates and officeholders choose not to be constrained by truth and reality, especially if those things threaten to get in the way of winning the argument.

Second, the vicious tone further hinders progress on key issues. Many appear unable to separate passion for an issue with disgust for anyone who holds a different view on that issue. Not only do individuals attack one another, but they do so in grossly exaggerated terms. A US representative may raise a perfectly reasonable question about, for instance, the Keystone Pipeline only to have her loyalty to her party stridently questioned. A US senator returns from the US-Mexico border advocating for more humane treatment of those being detained and gets labeled as weak on national security.

Third, indirect speech, sometimes referred to as "dog whistles," uses coded phrases in political messaging to reassure certain constituencies that the person speaking stands with them, even if the position is morally questionable or ethically deplorable. People accused President Trump of inciting white supremacists groups with his dog whistles during his first presidential campaign and following Charlottesville, but he is not the only public figure who messages in this way, nor is it done only by the Republican Party. Many groups communicate with their own coded language and thinly sliced words, sending messages to hold political camps together and reassure voters and donors that the candidate or elected leader understands and supports their particular concerns.

Fourth, some people attempt to fool us into thinking a serious debate is going on when really few great debates about things that affect people's lives are occurring on any level. The loud, out-of-control panelists on news networks can make it seem otherwise, but more often than not they are suppressing or redirecting a conversation rather than actually fostering and participating in one. The same goes for social media where posts at first can appear to put forward the merits of a given position, but frequently deteriorate into a malicious excoriation of people who hold a different view on that issue. This, of course, shuts down the possibility of dialogue, learning, and progress.

## Why This Issue Matters

It feels trite for me to write about why this issue matters, but I don't think everyone appreciates the kind of political cliff we are approaching as long as the four examples above continue to undermine honest debates and truthful conversations. So, I'll make a case for why this matters and trust that you will make your own.

The Democratic-controlled House of Representatives passed over four hundred bills during 2019, but most of those died on Senator Mitch McConnell's desk without any consideration or deliberation. Many of the stalled bills carry bipartisan support and address issues that make a difference in the everyday lives of people, such as proposed legislation concerning violence against women, net neutrality, and background checks. McConnell has referred to himself as "the grim reaper" of potential legislation, but he actually moves rather quickly with things that interest him, like approving federal judges. This occurs despite the American Bar Association raising serious concerns about the integrity, professional competence, and judicial temperament of many of those recent nominees.

So, just allowing debate to occur would be a good first step, but of course, a fruitful debate depends on honesty. Posturing, grandstanding, exaggerating, and caricaturing do not bear fruit. A difference exists, or at least should exist, between a speech on the

Senate or House floor and a person's next campaign commercial. Floating ideas and conspiracy theories to scare people is no way to govern or campaign. The really unmoored and reckless voices have learned that some people will eventually believe a lie if they keep saying it over and over, adding volume each time. It's not that the lie ever becomes truth, but that over time people come to the conclusion, "There must be something to that or we wouldn't still be hearing about it."

Truth is grounded in the soil of recognized facts, mutually affirmed stories, common commitments, and shared dreams, but today it seems that truth is another item in the marketplace. Truth has become that which can garner the most votes, sell the most products, and build the best reputation, even if no shred of facts, commitments, and dreams can be discerned.

I understand that entering into any debate involves the risk of losing the argument and not achieving the outcome that I most desire. It's something we learn in elementary school, usually on the same day that teachers tell us about the power of the compromise. A heated, honest debate can lead to a constructive compromise in which all sides contribute something that helps move the conversation forward and set it up for the next incremental, positive development.

In this model, we benefit from diverse perspectives, from truth spoken in love, and from a deep desire to solve problems, ease suffering, and enhance the quality of life for all of us. However, if either of us is so concerned about what we might lose or, worse, who might get the credit, problems fester, suffering increases, and the deterioration of our shared life accelerates.

## The Witness of the Church

The church has its own issues when it comes to engaging in authentic and serious debates, not the least of which is extreme avoidance, but Alasdair MacIntyre contends that a story is never more alive than when its characters are rigorously sorting out the values, priorities, and goods of that story. So many mainstream churches coasted along for a good while with the support of our culture and, as a result, never had to articulate and claim their values and priorities, but that day is over. How we go about describing beliefs, practices, and mission of the church will not be easy work. Some won't know where to start, and once we start we will find it to be a messy process. We likely will encounter surprises as people with whom we worshipped for years express views that are quite different from our own.

And yet, this is not only an opportunity for us to rediscover our identity and calling as the church, it also provides a timely and compelling mode for the wider community of what deep, serious, and honest debate looks like. As we "argue it out,"[1] to quote Isaiah, we bear witness to a way of approaching difficult issues that casts no one aside while remaining in a discerning position to listen for the Spirit's leading.

Bountiful and effective resources exist for such a process, including *7 Principles of Fierce Conversation*,[2] by Susan Scott, and *How the Body of Christ Talks*,[3] by Chris Smith. What is missing more often than techniques and information is the nerve to begin an important, albeit difficult, conversation. Scripture, though, calls us to let the same mind be in us that was in Christ Jesus.[4] That will involve effort, discernment, discomfort, and the belief that something good will come from the process. The spirit with which we go about such a process can shine a light for those trying to find their way in other conversations.

Honest engagement involves coming face to face with each other. It also means that we listen and talk with those with whom we disagree—sometimes vehemently disagree. And that is exactly the order prescribed in that well-known passage from Ecclesiastes

1. Isa 1:18. It's interesting how various translations seem to have pitched the rigor of such encounters. The King James Version, in all its poetic genteelness, invites us to "come now, and let us reason together." The New International Version seeks to resolve things when it implores us to "come now, let us settle the matter."

2. See Scott, *Fierce Conversations*.

3. See Smith, *How the Body of Christ Talks*.

4. Phil 2:5.

that promises that there is a time for everything and a season for every activity under the heavens. "There is a time to be silent and a time to speak."[5] The verse says we are silent first. Or, as the Prayer of St. Francis implores, "Grant that I may not so much seek . . . to be understood as to understand."[6]

We resist the silence because we fear we may lose something and we fail to trust the good that can come from attempting to understand each other. Whether across the aisle in a legislative chamber, or across the cabinet table in the White House, or across a dinner table at a family gathering, or around the Communion Table at church, more possibilities exist and more positive impact can be realized when we dare to be honest in both our listening and in our speech.

"Because at Costco, we clap for the truth." That can be our witness as the church. We can clap for the truth. We can raise our voices and cast our votes in protest when no truth can be found. And we can model what a thoughtful, mutual pursuit of truth looks like. Doing so gives us the best chance at observing and participating in honest debates and real conversations.

Ready to clap at the sound of truth,
Bill

---

5. Eccl 3:7b.

6. This prayer is attributed to St. Francis of Assisi, though its origins are not completely certain.

## Questions for Discussion

1. What current issue or situation needs our urgent attention and honest debate?

2. What information do you most need in order to feel prepared for an honest debate about the issue or situation you just named, and from where will that support, resources, training, or spiritual strength come?

3. To what extent will the perceived capacity of candidates to engage in honest, real conversations with voters influence your participation in the 2020 US election?

## 13

# For Clarity between Ethical
# Commitments and Political Advantage

My Sisters and Brothers,

TO IMPEACH A PRESIDENT is a significant event. To remove a president from office is almost unimaginable. The thought of doing so gave me, and I assume most people, very serious pause. Because impeachment is such a serious matter, it calls for the fairest investigation possible, full disclosure of the facts, honest representation of those facts, and profound impartiality. And as is the case with most complex, hotly contested situations, those who are directly involved jockey for political advantage while navigating—or avoiding—numerous ethical issues and implications.

On the day after the Senate found President Trump not guilty in its impeachment trial, Senator McConnell said that the House Democrats had made "a colossal political mistake." I agree with Senator McConnell and I hope you will stay with me long enough to hear why I hold that view.

This country knew some of the worst things we can know about a human being when it elected Donald Trump as president. He ran on an "antiestablishment, above-the-law, rules-don't-apply-to-me" platform and won. A lot of people believed that our political system, especially at the federal level, badly needed shaking up. Many who voted for candidate Trump did so for that reason alone. It was time, as the candidate himself put it, to drain the swamp. Many voted for him despite his caustic, vulgar rhetoric, lack of political experience, and vaguely defined plans for the country's direction—or perhaps because of those things!

When such qualities characterize the election, what leverage is there after that? The road to acquittal in the Senate was paved with the stones of a campaign and an administration that announced its disregard for laws and decorum from the start. And now, the most serious recourse we have—the impeachment of a president—proves that he is untouchable. He now heads into the 2020 campaign having received his highest approval rating (a modest 49%) during the impeachment process.

I realize that by the time this book finds its way into print a lot may have changed about this situation, but as I write this in mid-February 2020 I believe that impeaching the president likely will turn out to be a political mistake. President Trump has a baffling yet uncanny ability to convert horrendously embarrassing news and events about himself into political advantage. How can an allegedly prosperous businessperson who on his first run for political office won the US presidency so capably and comfortably assume the role of victim? I don't know, but we now have seen it happen numerous times on the most public stage of all. Scandals and controversies fly around him, but the worse the charges, the larger his political rallies are across the country.

## Why This Issue Matters

Whether the impeachment was a political mistake really is not my main question or concern. What I want to believe to be the bigger question is whether it was an ethical mistake.

Congress faced an incredibly difficult decision upon learning that the president withheld congressionally approved funds to support Ukraine's ongoing stabilizing efforts until the Ukrainian president agreed to announce an investigation into Trump's political rival, Joe Biden. What options existed for Congress as it sought to fulfill its responsibilities? And within those options, where did the needle fall between ethical commitments and political advantage?

First, the House of Representatives could have ignored the situation completely, even to the extent of not mentioning it in the upcoming presidential campaign. However, is it ethical to not investigate the possibility of wrongdoing when people level credible charges? And in this age, when at least part of the political equation turns on highlighting serious shortcomings of one's opponents, to remain silent during the campaign season about the charges brought against the president does not seem like a politically advantageous strategy. The House leadership did not choose this path.

Second, the House of Representatives could have publicized the president's actions, but not pursued any congressional action toward the president. Instead, they would make it a campaign issue with the hope that voters would be outraged by what the president did. Knowing the Republican majority in the Senate and the enthusiastic support President Trump commands there, the likelihood of the Senate removing Trump from office was very, very slim. In this scenario, the Democrats' best hope was to defeat Trump in November. Nor did the House leadership choose this path.

Third, the House leadership apparently believed that the ethical considerations of this situation demanded making formal charges against the president, even if doing so backfired politically against those bringing the charges. One option was to censure the president. This public reprimand by the House of Representatives would have been seen by some to fulfill ethical obligations and responsibilities, on the one hand, while also posturing for political advantage on the other. President Andrew Jackson was censured in 1834 for withholding documents from a congressional investigation, so the parallel between that situation and the current one puts the House leadership on solid ground to consider censure. However, the House leadership must have believed that censure simply did not sufficiently address what they viewed as the president's wrongdoing. The House leadership did not choose to censure the president.

In the end, the House leadership believed that the evidence legally and ethically required them to begin an impeachment process. The House Managers surely knew this would be an intense, messy process with many barriers and obstacles, but they pursued the investigation and charged the president with abuse of power and obstruction of Congress. Additional evidence surfaced even as the Senate voted on the two articles of impeachment. The House leadership pressed the point that this was an ethical matter from which they could not turn away and still fulfill their oath of office. So, they pursued impeachment.

Or—and we have to be realistic about this—the House leadership believed that combining an impeachment process with a hard-hitting campaign against the president provided them with the greatest political advantage. In other words, perhaps this scenario features both ethical commitments and political advantages. I don't know the weight they assigned or did not assign to the political ramifications of such a move, but they had to know political risks were involved. And yet, whatever the gains or threats, they believed the ethical course of action was to investigate this matter and to go where the investigation led.

As a result of the president's ability to spin news about him in an unbelievably positive light among his supporters, the narrative from the impeachment process that the president has fostered and that most of his followers accept is that the House Democrats, still stinging from the 2016 election, made a reckless, time-consuming, partisan attempt to make the president look unpopular and corrupt as he approaches reelection. In an atrociously ironic move, the narrative also compares this process with the Clinton impeachment and cites how they both were politically motivated. Between the president's ability to control the narrative, the traction this narrative is gaining, the improved approval ratings of the president, and the president's increasingly emboldened rhetoric and actions, I believe the impeachment process backfired politically. To the extent that is true, Senator McConnell is right. It was a colossal political mistake.

I also believe pursuing impeachment was the ethical thing to do. And sometimes doing the right thing carries political costs and disadvantages.

## The Witness of the Church

The witness of the church includes the ideas that truth matters, that neighborly love is our calling, and that God's dream for the world is characterized by a shalom in which all the people of the earth experience well-being and deep, lasting justice. Scripture offers various ways for us to understand and embody an ethical life, reminding us that ethical positions do not always put us at a political advantage. Jesus' own execution is an example of that. He might have avoided death on the cross by being less strident in his speech and action, but his love for the ways of God put him not only at further political disadvantage, but also in harm's way.

Scripture's ethical mandates address our speech, our conduct, relationships, how we live in the world, and how we discern a faithful way in complicated and messy situations. In other words, Scripture can guide our discernment of ethical considerations, commitments, and actions as we work through difficult realities, including political ones like an impeachment process. In community with one another, we bring the lens of faith to bear on complex issues and situations with the hope of sorting out what is right and what is expedient and popular.

With our speech, Jesus urged us to let our yes be yes, and our no, no.[1] Truth-telling not only forms the basis for an honest conversation and relationship, it also reveals certain things and makes other things possible. As we share life with one another, our truth-telling helps us understand more about what it means to be a community together.

---

1. Matt 5:37.

With regard to how we show up as our true selves, Scripture strikes a complementary chord between living with strong convictions and practicing genuine humility. For example, Jesus speaks boldly to his own community about the weightier matters of the law—justice, mercy, and faith[2]—and then washes his friends' feet later. Strong convictions and deep humility comprise an important part of an ethical vision for the world.

With regard to our relationships, we know that it is always wrong to treat people badly, period. Jesus spoke both of love of neighbor and love of enemy. He called people beyond comfort zones and social conventions to relationships of care, mutuality, and trust. Paul encouraged Christians to be kind and tenderhearted toward each other, saying that doing those things with each other would remind us of our relationship with God.[3]

We honor the worth and dignity of every person with how we live in this beautiful and extravagantly diverse world. We affirm that we are all part of the family of God. As a colleague said to me, "God does not create 'thems.'" We may try to draw lines, pass laws, and turn the public against some groups of people, but that is our doing, not God's.

The country needed to know whether and to what extent the president violated trust and laws when he withheld aid to Ukraine, so the House leadership undertook not just the pursuit of information, but of truth. In doing so, political realities hung in the balance, as they often do. Our own commitment to the kind of community that Jesus envisioned is a comment to truth, to honest and authentic relationships, to a community characterized by convictions and humility, and to bending the country toward fairness, integrity, and an ethical commitment that dares to risk political disadvantage for the common good.

This is not new to the church. It is the witness of the church—to embody first the ethical vision we want to see in the world and then to partner with God and each other in the making of that ethical world, even though at times it, no doubt, will leave us at

2. Matt 23:23.
3. Eph 4:32.

a political disadvantage. But, regardless of how many crosses the empires of the world raise on Golgotha, a resurrection power is still at work. It may not win the next election, but it will never stop inviting us toward the kind of world that Jesus describes.

People have framed this chapter of the Trump presidency in lots of ways. But Jesus and his followers must frame it as an ethical issue.

Hoping ethical commitments win the day,
Bill

## Questions for Discussion

1. Do you believe impeaching President Trump was the right course of action, even if it carries political disadvantages? Why or why not?

2. What are the lingering effects, if any, of the impeachment process among the people with whom you live, work, play, and worship?

3. What ethical commitments do you want to see enacted by our elected leaders?

4. To what extent will the ethical commitments of presidential candidates influence your participation in the 2020 election?

## 14

# To Abide in an Unfailing Center
# in the Midst of Change

My Sisters and Brothers,

WE CREDIT HERACLITUS WITH the observation that the only constant thing is change, though it's hard to imagine what similarities exist between our time and his world of 500 BCE. Ray Kurzweil, on the other hand, is a well-known futurist living today. His comparison between linear growth and exponential growth at least confirms why many of us feel so decentered so much of the time. Kurzweil said, "30 steps linearly gets you to 30. One, two, three, four, and with step 30 you're at 30. With exponential growth, it's one, two, four, eight and with step 30, you're at a billion."[1]

Things especially change quickly in areas like communication, medicine, climate, technology, population shifts, political alliances, international boundaries, and commerce. Education, law, social work, accounting, engineering, and a hundred other fields struggle to keep up. Dozens of new fields exist now that did not exist a decade ago, but the real news may be that most of the jobs that people will hold twenty years from now do not exist yet today. Change is occurring so fast that, when measured against the pace

1. Kurzweil, "Breakfast with the Financial," interview, April 10, 2015.

of change in previous eras, Kurzweil says that change in the twenty-first century will equal twenty thousand years of what might be considered a more normal pace of change. Generally, ethicists are always trying to catch up with the changes and articulate what represents life-giving decisions and actions in various fields.

## Why This Issue Matters

We spend our days trying not to become completely unmoored from what grounds us and helps us live well in the world. To play with Jesus' words a bit from the Sermon on the Mount, we may well have followed the wise man's example and built our house—or our lives—on the rock, but it too often feels like someone replaced our foundation of rock with shifting sand and left us vulnerable to all sorts of howling winds.[2] The experience leaves us wondering if there is anything upon which we might rebuild our lives that won't change or erode.

Others know a different experience. It's one of great discovery and perpetual adventure, often driven (but not always) by a deep desire to address individual and societal challenges. Fiercely committed women and men recognize the inequities of the status quo and work daily on changing systems that keep people down and lock people out. Deeply passionate people identify cracks in the system where individuals and whole communities regularly fall through and never recover their previous lives. Wonderfully gifted people spend hours in research and development for the next critical cure, the next less-invasive procedure and the next compatible therapy that improves and even restores quality of life.

All of these are changes of one kind or another. All of them touch real lives, as well as pose ethical considerations. We try to balance our hopefulness about some changes with a persistent uncertainty about what other changes are coming our way. Along the way, we also deal with what seem at best to be silly changes for change's sake. I will never understand why my bank replaced

2. Matt 7:24–27.

its ATM with a new model that requires four more steps for every transaction than the old one, but I am moved to thanksgiving and appreciation when I think of the changes that will enhance the lives of many people and, hopefully, inspire the rest of us to participate in changes worth pursuing and making.

## The Witness of the Church

Scripture rarely speaks more eloquently or movingly than in those times when change and uncertainty grip the people. "The Lord is my shepherd"[3] registers in the hospital room and at the gravesite with the promise of God's presence and guidance in the same deep and comforting way that it did for the psalmist. "Peace I leave with you; my peace I give to you. I do not give as the world gives. Do not let your hearts be troubled, and do not let them be afraid"[4] resonates at every moment of transition, just as it did when Jesus bid his disciples farewell. "Where can I go from your Spirit, or where can I flee from your presence"[5] assures us that God holds us wherever we are and wherever we go.

These words from Psalm 46 speak clearly and hopefully into experiences and emotions that we know all too well.

> God is our refuge and strength,
> a very present help in trouble.
> Therefore we will not fear, though
> the earth should change,
> though the mountains shake
> in the heart of the sea;
> though its waters roar and foam,
> though the mountains tremble
> with its tumult.
> God is in the midst of the city;
> it shall not be moved;
> God will help it when the

---

3. Ps 23.
4. John 14: 27.
5. Ps 139:7.

morning dawns.
The nations are in an uproar,
the kingdoms totter
he utters his voice, the earth melts.
The Lord of hosts is with us;
the God of Jacob is our refuge.
Be still, and know that I am God.[6]

Even amid political calamity when it feels like the earth is moving beneath our feet, God is present. To paraphrase Yeats, even when things are falling apart and the center does not hold, even when anarchy is loosed upon the world,[7] God is in our midst. Even when situations become so unpredictable that the trouble feels to us like the mountains shaking in the heart of the sea, God's help is near. Even when nations are in uproar, like ours seems to be right now, the voice of God calms the trembling so that we can breathe again in hope and confidence.

The psalmist offers a new dimension of encouragement by saying that God is "in the midst of the city." It might prove comforting just to know that God occasionally thinks about where we are. Still another level of comfort would come with the news that God watches over our lives. The psalmist assures us of something more. God is near, so close that God feels the trouble and the trembling and yet remains with us through the uproar. This allows us to remain in our settings as well, trusting God's voice and working for good in the midst of the most challenging of circumstances, including situations made far worse by shortsightedness of policy, meanness of spirit, erratic behavior, and extremist ideology. It is easy to make the turmoil worse, especially when self-promoting leaders cleverly escalate the fear to throw us into a state of reactivity and then swoop into promise they are the only ones who can help us.

God abides with us, always. God is faithful. Surely we believe that, wherever we find ourselves on the political or theological spectrum and whatever our social location is. Though I don't always know what understanding of God people are invoking when

6. Ps 46:1–3, 5–7, 10a.

7. Yeats, "The Second Coming."

they spew hate and encourage violence with their explicit rhetoric and their dog whistles, perhaps one of the few things we can all agree on is the faithfulness of God. God infuses the world with goodness and healing. When we do not or cannot accept that goodness and healing, God calls to us in the messy circumstances we have created either with our intentions or our finitude, sets before us "life and death, blessings and curses,"[8] and implores us to choose life, for our sake and for the sake of all whom God cherishes. We are God's beloved, all of us. God does not forsake God's own beloved, whatever the changes around may bring.

God abides with us. And we abide in God. In God, "we live and move and have our being."[9] The meaning, purpose, and contribution of our lives arise from our life in God. God envelopes us with grace, centers us with peace, and focuses our lives so that we are not perpetually thrown off balance with the latest surprise in the news, development in a political proceeding, or act of violence in the community.

And when we abide in God, we abide in love, not fear. We abide in community, not isolation. We abide in integrity, not dishonesty. We abide in humility, not bombast. We abide in common celebration and struggle, not only in individual accomplishments and private security. We abide in an atmosphere of radical hospitality, not in a closed system that comes up with its own reasons as to why some people should not be accepted and honored for who they are. When we abide in God, we not only abide in the Light, but we become light to the world around us, a light that invites others to join us in our abiding in God and God abiding with us.

Of all the times and ways when we are feeling disconnected from one another and even from our truest selves, the temptation is to disconnect from the church, from the community where we are known and loved. And the church itself faces this temptation. The church can get strangely separated from its own faith story and unable or disinterested in accessing God's gifts of hope and peace, joy and love. In other words, for all its talk about God in hymns and

8. Deut 30:19.
9. Acts 17:28.

prayers and sermons, the church doesn't always abide in God and instead tries to build a life on the same shifting sands that we have found so unfulfilling and unreliable in the rest of our lives.

To abide is to trust and to act on that trust. To trust God is to trust in the purposes of God that have been revealed to us through the bold themes of Scripture, the prophets of then and now, and, especially, through the life of Jesus of Nazareth. God desires and asks of us a love of neighbor that moves well beyond neutrality and even fondness and participates in the making of a community where people can be called to a flourishing and hopeful life. God desires and asks of us such a passion for fairness and justice that we bring all who have been left out and left behind into that flourishing, hopeful life.

God desires and asks of us to live in covenant with all of creation—air, water, soil, animals, woods, rivers, streams, and all the resources we don't regularly notice but nonetheless remain essential to a sustainable ecosystem—so that we can live well and responsibly on the earth. God desires and asks of us a humility that causes us to think and act with one eye toward the circumstances immediately before us and with one toward the eternal horizon of God's good will, thus not falling prey to knee-jerk decisions fueled by anxiety, political pressure, or personal gain.

We are especially likely to awaken to God's presence in times of great change, but God invites us in every season to abide in divine love and purpose. We do so through our meditation and prayer, as well as through our service and generosity. We abide in God in the personal times of stillness and vulnerability, and when we join in worship and study through the community of Jesus' friends we call the church. As the psalmist promises, God is always in our midst.

Abiding in God with you,
Bill

## Questions for Discussion

1. If you were to name only one from all the changes you have seen or experienced, what change in the church or culture has been the most difficult for you to understand, live with, resist, or embrace?

2. How does your faith help you live with change?

3. To what extent will a candidate's ability to demonstrate stability and sustain proper focus influence your participation in the 2020 US election?

What We Are Called To

## 15

# To Share in Acts of Confession, Vocation, and Justice

My Sisters and Brothers,

I WAS A GUEST preacher at a church once on the Sunday nearest the Fourth of July. It's fairly common for ministers to avoid that Sunday by taking a week of vacation. During worship, a distinguished-looking man in a dark suit with gray hair and designer eyeglasses stood at the pulpit and read, first, the opening sentences of the Declaration of Independence and then, the Preamble to the Constitution. I thought for sure we were headed toward the Pledge of Allegiance, but we will never know. The man became so emotional as he concluded the Preamble that he walked quickly to his seat, profusely wiping his eyes. I learned later from a lengthy conversation with him that his tears were prompted by pride and gratitude for his country.

Later that same week, I attended a community mobilization meeting geared toward providing safe passage for political and economic refugees seeking to enter the United States at the US-Mexico border. Several in the crowd knew family members and friends who were trying to cross. Guards had detained some of their relatives immediately after they crossed. Guards turned away others completely and sent them into an unimaginable wilderness. The speakers recounted these and other atrocities that our country has visited upon people over the course of our history. As people spoke, many around me profusely wiped tears of grief and terror from their eyes. Same country, same week, very different feelings.

Toni Morrison once described three things that groups share in common, no matter how vastly different their other views, positions, and beliefs may be. She said those three things are community, eternity, and exclusion. Then she explained those three things in shorthand: "you and me together, forever, without them."[1] Community is about you and me. Eternity is forever. Exclusion, a trait that Morrison says all groups share, loves the idea of community and eternity, but *without them*. That sentiment represents too much of our national and church history.

## Why This Issue Matters

This matters for several reasons. First, we have not always done right by people on this continent and we have often not owned up to that. Too many Americans are invisible in their own country. Their faces go unseen and their stories go unheard. When they receive notice or mention, it often takes the form of degrading comments.

Second, for all our flaws and missteps, the principles and commitments of the United States are still worth preserving. We just need to do a better job of embracing those commitments. "We the people" should mean *we the people*, no matter who is uttering that phrase. The American dream should not be fairly attainable for some and an utter nightmare for others.

Third, we should act before it is too late. I do not believe our country has a future of strength and promise in its current state of willful polarization and wedge-issue politics. We cannot continue to swing back and forth, demanding that our extremes get implemented after we win elections while obstructing and tearing apart the other side as they attempt to govern after we lose. At this point,

1. Hilton, *House United*, 60.

it may take something catastrophic to recover a kinder, more constructive political atmosphere. I hope not, but I think it's quite possible. The church will not reverse this situation on its own, but it can contribute positively. As Sandhya Jha writes, "We are not in the days of Franco's Spain or Vichy France, but we are now in times when, to paraphrase Pastor Trocme, our individual and community efforts to do small acts of resistance and hope and accountability either with or as people on the margins are necessary."[2]

## The Witness of the Church—Confession

A confession from *Enriching Our Worship* says, "We repent of the evil that enslaves, the evil we have done, and the evil done on our behalf."[3] It's a startling confession intended to dislodge us from anyone trapped in privilege and denial.

I am well acquainted with those first two evils. I also know that I am complicit in systems that wreak havoc—and yes, evil—on people's lives, but just acknowledging that on an intellectual level and going on with life as I know it doesn't change anything. However, publicly confessing that third phrase on my knees over many years caused me to confront that very uncomfortable reality in a new way. I can continue to say that I never owned slaves, turned away a political refugee, or built a nuclear warhead, but evil has been done and is being done on my behalf and our behalf. Some things need to be confessed, over and over again. We cannot casually speak of them as if we are not connected to them just because we didn't wield the whip or build the wall or assemble the missile.

Some denominations have confessed their complicity and sought to move forward in a more just and humble manner. For example, the Church of the Brethren included a confession when it restated its historic opposition to slavery, saying, "We confess our complicity in the global network of slavery through consumption of goods and services that have been produced by slave labor.

2. Jha, *Transforming Communities*, 143.
3. Episcopal Church, *Enriching Our Worship*, 19.

We commit to educating ourselves and others about modern-day slavery and initiating and supporting antislavery action at home and abroad."[4] Of course, that's a slightly easier confession to make when your church has been expressing its opposition to slavery since 1782.

The Southern Baptist Convention acknowledged that its "relationship to African Americans has been hindered from the beginning by the role that slavery played in the formation of the Southern Baptist Convention." The resolution apologized "to all African Americans for condoning and/or perpetuating individual and systemic racism in our lifetime," repented of conscious and unconscious racism, acknowledged that the healing of the SBC and its members was at stake, and committed themselves to eradicate racism in all its forms from Southern Baptist life and ministry.[5]

This is a moment in the life of our country to confess our own direct acts of evil, as well as evil done on our behalf. It's also another moment that calls for action.

## The Witness of the Church—Vocation

Vocation is central to the Christian story. We may experience a call from God in different ways, but as long as pain and injustice exist in the world God will continue to call to you and me and the church to respond.

Sometimes, that call comes through concrete circumstances that cannot stand. People awaken to what is afoot and courageous leadership rises in surprising and compelling ways. For example, that's how the movement Black Lives Matter emerged. Three women came together in 2013 in response to the acquittal of Trayvon Martin's murderer, George Zimmerman. When Michael Brown was killed the following year in Ferguson, Missouri, the movement focused on supporting the protesters in Ferguson and prepared for other situations that, tragically, would call out for their presence.

4. Church of the Brethren, "Statements on Slavery."

5. All quotes in this paragraph are from the Southern Baptist Convention, "Resolution on Racial Reconciliation."

Protesters came from across the country to stand with the people of Ferguson and then returned to their communities to begin eighteen new chapters of Black Lives Matter. Organizers Alicia Garza, Patrisse Cullors, and Opal Tometi sought to make visible a situation that much of our country found very difficult to look at without becoming extremely uncomfortable. It creates great discomfort to realize how many people and groups go unseen and unnoticed, but without a jolting disruption to the way we see our own country we likely will continue policies and positions that benefit only a portion of our people.

## The Witness of the Church—Justice

The possibility of reparations has been debated occasionally in some circles, but has not consistently gained widespread traction. The prophets call us to correct oppression, to pursue justice and righteousness, and to repair the breach.[6] Institutions of higher education usually take a conservative approach to their finances, often to their own detriment. When well-heeled institutions take steps toward reparations, it catches our attention. Two prominent US seminaries announced reparative measures in 2019.

While several colleges and other schools have considered such a move, Virginia Theological Seminary set aside $1.7 million for a slavery reparations fund. The money is intended to encourage more African Americans to consider ministry in the Episcopal Church and to serve directly the needs of any descendants of the enslaved Africans who helped build the VTS campus in Alexandria, Virginia. VTS did not admit students of color until the 1950s. While testifying at a congressional hearing that reparations are about more than monetary compensation, Bishop Eugene Sutton of the Episcopal Diocese of Maryland said, "An act of reparations is an attempt to make whole again, to restore, to offer atonement, to make amends, to reconcile for a wrong or an injury."[7]

6. Isa 1:17; Jer 22:3; Isa 58:12.
7. Paulsen, "$1.7 Million for Slavery Reparations Fund."

Less than a month after Virginia Theological Seminary set aside a reparations fund, Princeton Theological Seminary set aside nearly $28 million for scholarships and fellowships for descendants of people who were enslaved, as well as for others from underrepresented groups. This move comes after the seminary investigated its relationship to slavery. Interestingly, the report found that the seminary did not own slaves and that its buildings were not constructed with slave labor.

However, the school did receive financial support from Southern sources, including slave owners and congregations with ties to slavery. For a time, a large portion of the seminary's endowment was connected to Southern banks that were financing the expansion of slavery.[8] In other words, Princeton Seminary took reparative steps for the evil done on its behalf, even if it did not directly participate in the act of owning slaves or exploiting slave labor.

These efforts are beginning points. Some, no doubt, will criticize parts of these plans, but I believe a beginning point is something upon which we can build.

Repairing the breach with you,
Bill

## Questions for Discussion

1. For what transgression do you believe the church or the country should confess its sin and apologize to those who have been or continue to be harmed by policies or actions?

2. What form, if any, should reparations take in the example you named in the question above?

3. What does your desire for hope and healing cause you to think and do during the 2020 US campaign and election?

8. The Princeton report is quoted in Kaur, "New Jersey Religious College."

## 16

# To Think Carefully and Critically

My Sisters and Brothers,

EVERYONE HAS OPINIONS—AND A right to those opinions—but
many of those opinions are little more than reactions. With all the
uncertainty, anxiety, and fear at play that we discussed earlier, we
react to each other, often in a quickly antagonistic manner, rather
than reason together.

People often can name what they like and what they don't
like, which is important, but are unable to say why they like or dislike something. As a result, we cannot enter into fruitful exchanges
with one another that otherwise could lead to understanding and
clarification, both for our own positions and those of other people.

This happens all across the political and theological spectrum. We are more inclined to move away from each other rather
than toward each other. We seek to protect our unconsidered
views on various issues. And when someone attempts to engage
in thoughtful dialogue across some difference, an intensity often
ensues that shuts down the conversation. After all, we hold our
positions deeply and fervently. We do not take challenges to our
positions well or lightly. We look for champions for our positions
on the public stage and we scorn and tear down anyone we perceive as a threat to those positions.

Why, then, do we hold the positions and opinions that we hold? Perhaps cultural pressure or party loyalty or loyalty to the president or another key public figure causes us to go along with something without giving it much thought. Perhaps grief grips us and we are unable to separate our emotion about a situation from its reality and the facts. Perhaps the media influences our thinking more than we admit, even to the point of crowding out one of the greatest of American virtues, which is independent thought.

Whether it's for one of these reasons or for something else, it is clear that our country suffers from a lack of both careful thinking and critical thinking. I like the example Lee Ramsey set when he spelled out the word careful to read "care-full" in the title of one of his books.[1] Care-full thinking breaks down barriers and strips away assumptions about each other so that we can come to have the mind of Christ in us, a mind characterized by humility and openness. Care-full thinking is slow thinking, attentive to details, precise in its descriptions and vigilant in its processing. Care-full thinking takes into consideration the goodwill we want to show toward other people so that, when we are talking with or about others, our speech reflects care and concern.

Critical thinking does not mean we are constantly criticizing things, but always examining our assumptions and logic about a position. We do so to understand more deeply the opportunities and challenges before us, to keep in check the reactionary defaults that run rampant in our culture and deepen the messes in which we find ourselves. Critical thinking can prove to be an act of resistance when, to paraphrase Kipling, people all about us are losing their heads and yet blaming it on us.[2]

Daniel Kahneman captures an important dimension of critical thinking when he describes the difference between what he calls system-one thinking and system-two thinking.[3] System one, which is the system operating in our culture right now, cannot get enough information. With a voracious appetite, system one takes

1. See Ramsey, *Care-full Preaching*.
2. Kipling, "If," 170.
3. See Kahneman, *Thinking Fast and Slow*.

in everything around it and, with very little processing, quickly forms impressions and feelings about what it sees and hears. System one will bend any new information to fit with what it already believes to be true. Does this sound familiar?

System two, on the other hand, works more slowly, parsing data, analyzing arguments, and understanding situations. Unfortunately, system two is lazy. It does not kick in on its own and, when it does boot up, it can be frustratingly slow. System two considers evidence, questions assumptions, and, based on what is discovered in that process, decides on a path forward and then acts in that direction. Our country could use more system-two thinking.

## Why This Issue Matters

Though the greatest commandment tells us to love God with our minds, our political environment undercuts that at every turn. To love God with our minds involves exercising curiosity, assessing situations, articulating values, and developing constructive ways forward together. Many have given up on this process, largely because they already have formed their positions. They know that the discovery of any information or the revisiting of current information can be risky. In an era of extreme positions, people cannot reverse their convictions and still save face.

Careful and critical thinking leads to an examination of issues. Let's take immigration, for instance. If we only listen to those on the Left, we would assume that President Trump is the first to exercise extreme measures on the US/Mexican border, but that's not true. United States policies have been in place since at least the Carter presidency. Bill Ong Hing argues that militarization at the border began during the Clinton presidency. Forgotten in the narrative from this perspective completely is that President Obama, by his own admission, used tough immigration practices as a bargaining chip to bring Republicans to the table to develop lasting reform. Unfortunately, President Obama's record-setting deportations were not enough to entice the Republican leadership into a careful and critical conversation.[4] And, sadly, rarely is the debate about immigration framed by what the character of our country can and should be. More often, that debate revolves only around scarcity and safety.

In other cases, people we have entrusted with leadership take advantage of our lack of care-full and critical thinking and exploit the very people they represent. For example, Senate Majority Leader Mitch McConnell regularly rallied voters with his attacks on President Obama. McConnell especially crusaded against ObamaCare, referring to it as an unparalleled evil that needed to be repealed immediately. At the same time, however, he took credit for the large number of Americans who had secured health insurance through the exchanges made possible by the Affordable Care Act.

That's right, Senator McConnell campaigned for the repeal of ObamaCare and at the very same time lifted up the Affordable Care Act as a success, as if they were two different things! Senator McConnell knew that President Obama was very unpopular in parts of Kentucky, which by the way was largely the results of McConnell's efforts, so McConnell tapped into that dislike of Obama and rallied his constituents around the idea of repealing ObamaCare. He conveniently forgot to mention that many of them would lose their health insurance if his crusade was successful. Simply put, he was urging people to vote against their own best interests and have their healthcare taken away from them.

Some will label careful, critical thinking as elitist, especially those who have adopted anti-intellectualism in order to protect their prejudices and practices from self-examination and community accountability. Critical thinking isn't elitist or East Coast or anything else. I've witnessed people of all educational levels exercise critical thinking on matters related to their work, the land, their families, their faith, and community leadership. It's not elitist to articulate concepts thoughtfully and to debate ideas rigorously. Doing those things is a path toward achieving and living in the common good. And yet, the very exchanges that could lower the

---

4. Hing, *American Presidents*, 53–220.

temperature in our political environment and ease the suffering of the voiceless and forgotten never develop.

Why would we do this? We are smarter and wiser than we show. I know that not everybody believes that, but I do. We are more capable and insightful than our words and actions demonstrate, but we seem eager to put on display and into the public discourse the crudest, least thought-through, and most narrow-minded positions and ideas that can cross human lips. And it's killing us as a country.

## The Witness of the Church

The Apostle Paul might just as easily have been writing to us in our time as to Christians in Rome during his own time. "Do not be conformed to this world, but be transformed by the renewing of your minds" (Rom 12:2).

It makes rather obvious sense that the renewing of our minds will play a key role in our processing of information, pursuit of the truth, and problem-solving, but Paul makes a larger claim about the renewal of our minds. He says it will be the means of our transformation. Our thinking will change us for the good, Paul contends.

It seems almost naïve all these years later, but Paul thought that thinking was key for first-century Christians who lived daily with the oppression and violence of the Roman Empire. Empires minimize critical thinking. Crosses littered the Roman landscape with the hope that every execution served as a deterrent to the next person who dared to challenge the empire.

That makes Paul's rhetorical move all the more interesting in his Letter to the Romans. Paul first describes the world in which the church found itself, a world of brokenness, anxiety, and corruption. Then, beginning with chapter 12, Paul moves toward what a faithful life looks like in the new age of Jesus Christ. Ethical admonitions follow so that the early church could understand clearly the signs of this new age. Those ethical admonitions continue through the four remaining chapters, urging the Romans and us to "let love be genuine, hold fast to what is good, extend hospitality to strangers, bless those who persecute you, live in harmony with one another and overcome evil with good." Also included are things not to do, like not repaying evil for evil, or claiming to be wiser than we are, or avenging ourselves.[5]

Couched between Paul's description of a world in trouble and a list of ethical admonitions is a pivotal section that says, "Do not be conformed to this world, but be transformed by the renewing of your minds." That's how important and essential to the faith that Paul believed careful and critical thinking to be. Paul is saying that we will move from the way things are to the way God desires them to be through the renewal of our minds.

Our careful and critical thinking about our lives of faith, about the political climate in our country, and about the current religious environment will cause us to rise above the herd mentality and remain open to the new age of Jesus that is always trying to break into our midst and take hold. The renewal of our minds has a specific impact. In that new age, we challenge the empire with the will of God, a will which Paul describes as all those things that are "good and acceptable and perfect."[6]

When Paul was urging early Christians to claim new life by distinguishing themselves from their hostile, conflicted culture, he lifted up system-two virtues and made a bold promise. We take that promise to heart now, that we too will be transformed by the renewing of our minds.

Thinking carefully and critically with you,
Bill

---

5. Rom 12.
6. Rom 12:2.

## Questions for Discussion

1. In what ways do reason and critical thinking enhance how you experience God, deepen your understanding of the faith, and help you take your place in the world?

2. What are specific steps you can take in combatting the rampant anti-intellectualism in our country while at the same time staying connected to and working alongside people who may think that the "renewing of our minds" isn't important?

3. How will the significance you place on careful and critical thinking shape your participation in the 2020 US election?

# 17

# To Prepare for Conflict

My Sisters and Brothers,

IN 2015, I TOOK a group of seminary students to Selma, Alabama, for the fiftieth anniversary of Bloody Sunday. On March 7, 1965, several hundred people started across the Edmund Pettus Bridge on their way to Montgomery, marching for the right to vote. That attempt to cross the infamous bridge resulted in numerous life-threatening injuries as Alabama state police beat and kicked the marchers back across the bridge.

A second march two days later was aborted when Dr. Martin Luther King Jr. paused on the bridge, stared at the officers who again dared the marchers to attempt to cross, and then turned around and called off the march that day. Finally, on March 21, 1965, the marchers gathered again and this time walked across the Pettus Bridge and continued their fifty-four-mile trek on foot to Montgomery. Five months later, on August 6, 1965, President Lyndon B. Johnson signed the Voting Rights Act that granted all African Americans the right to vote. The journey was symbolic in some ways, but incredibly physical and political in others.

At the commemoration in 2015, President Obama offered soaring rhetoric and concrete examples at the foot of the Pettus Bridge, calling us to act on behalf of any who continue to be left out and left behind. Perhaps most striking of all was that President Obama was flanked by two people whose paths might never have crossed. One was Rep. John Lewis, who was nearly beaten to death by Alabama State Police officers on the marchers' first attempt across the Pettus Bridge. The other was Peggy Wallace Kennedy, the daughter of former Alabama governor George Wallace, who vehemently opposed racial desegregation in the South and who, tragically, found sympathetic ears in all parts of the country when he ran for president in 1968. In a remarkable development, Lewis and Kennedy are now friends who appear together to call the country to racial reconciliation. Later that day, Kennedy and Rev. Bernice King, Dr. King's youngest daughter, held hands as they retraced the steps of that Selma-to-Montgomery march.

It was an amazing experience in so many ways, but it was wrapped in realities that remind us that the march must continue. Our group spent most of that day in a part of Selma where it is difficult to detect that much progress has occurred in the last fifty years. Too many symbolic Pettus Bridges remain in this country. Some that once were destroyed are being revived and, incredibly, some new ones are being built, all of which diminish, discredit, and dismiss significant parts of our own American family.

Someone once told me in a very energized and concerned voice, "Bill, it's a battlefield out there. If you aren't preparing pastors, therapists, and community leaders for the battlefield, then I don't know what you are doing because the real world is a battlefield."

I pushed back on that. "Won't seeing everything as a battle bias and distort how we assess situations? Aren't we likely to limit what goes into our skill set and our toolbox if we believe every conversation, meeting, issue, and challenge is a battle?"

But I'm not sure I offered a credible challenge to his viewpoint, a viewpoint that he arrived at through experience that I do not have. You see, even in times when my lack of thought or care created hardship for myself, I still benefited from the privilege of growing up white, male, Christian, straight, middle-class, and with an extensive and reliable social safety net. Add to that a liberal Protestant background that left me with an incredibly underdeveloped concept of sin and it's no wonder that battlefield imagery did not resonate with me. I cannot appreciate the kinds of battles that people endure just to be seen, recognized, acknowledged, included, and appreciated. Those experiences of welcome ought to be givens, but they aren't. A whole other level of challenge comes when people must fight their way into systems and fight almost daily to keep their place in those systems.

## Why This Issue Matters

We can share in quaint conversations about justice without risking much of anything. We can join a study about justice where we amuse ourselves with stories from the past, hypothetical situations, and interesting religious ideas. We can observe justice and injustice from a safe distance. But while we do these things, we should not expect wrongs to be made right just because we are talking about these things or because time is passing.

Nor should we attempt to convince ourselves that our neutrality serves any honorable purpose. Silence always supports the status quo. Our efforts to hold a delicate balance or thread the needle on conflict in order to make the most people happy too often keeps unjust systems in place and enables prejudiced people and actions to continue. James Cone reminded us on that point, "There is no place in this war of liberation for nice white people who want to avoid taking sides and remain friends with both the racists and the Negro."[1] The same argument applies to other situations. Martin Niemöller, who as a pastor first supported the Nazi party before eventually resisting it and being imprisoned, said, "And here lies the real church problem. Nothing can be achieved by neutrals. They will evade all real decisions and will hinder all real activity in the Church."[2]

Martin Luther King Jr. said, "Human progress never rolls in on wheels of inevitability; it comes through the tireless efforts of

1. Cone, *Black Theology and Black Power*, 67.
2. Hockenos, *Then They Came for Me*, 172.

men willing to be co-workers with God, and without this hard work, time itself becomes an ally of the forces of social stagnation. We must use time creatively in the knowledge that the time is always ripe to do right."[3]

To do justice, as Scripture implores us to do,[4] means to engage what matters to us and, more importantly, what God desires for the world. And it will involve conflict. Defenders of the status quo sometimes will respond to our efforts with shame and aggression. The differences are real, the convictions are strong, the disregard for the truth is stunning, the lies and misinformation flood the system, the money is flowing like crazy, and people fear losing their power and control. We cannot live and work in an environment like that without facing conflict.

This is not news, or at least is shouldn't be. We surely have read Scripture's ironclad promises for Christians, but it may not have registered for us that, indeed, there will be times when we are not welcome,[5] encounter persecution,[6] find ourselves in conflict with those around us,[7] and experience religious and political resistance of various kinds and degrees.[8] Thankfully, Jesus does offer good news for those occasions: "Blessed are you when people revile you and persecute you and utter all kinds of evil against you falsely on my account. Rejoice and be glad, for your reward is great in heaven, for in the same way they persecuted the prophets who were before you."[9] The blessing is good news, but it's offered because in doing our part toward God's desired world we will face conflicts and some of those conflicts will be harsh and extreme.

There's a cost to speaking up and engaging, and there's a cost to being silent and not getting involved. We decide which price we are willing to pay and what outcome most closely aligns with

3. King, *Why We Can't Wait*, 74.

4. Micah 6:8.

5. Matt 10:14.

6. 1 Tim 3:12.

7. Matt 10:35.

8. Matt 9:10–13 and 21:1–11.

9. Matt 5:12.

what God desires for the world. Our country needs thoughtful, prayerful, discerning, and engaged people to participate in election cycles and in the issues that ripen in between those elections.

## The Witness of the Church

Many people picture the Pettus Bridge in their minds when they think of the struggle for civil rights and the march to Montgomery. That same bridge comes to mind every time a legislature or a court or an executive reverses or hollows out the provisions of prior accomplishments. In doing so, they undercut the work of those marchers and set back both the clock and the country.

But what often goes unnoticed or even unknown, especially by white Americans, is that the Pettus Bridge represents the second point for those marches. It was not the starting point. People came to Selma from all over the country to stand and march for the voting rights of African Americans, but when they arrived in Selma they didn't report to the bridge. They gathered first at a church. When would-be marchers came to Selma, their first stop was at the historic Brown Chapel, AME. You may have seen it portrayed well in the powerful movie *Selma*.

It was an amazing day to be at the Pettus Bridge on March 7, 2015, but to follow in the footsteps of heroic marchers, before we went to that bridge we went to Brown Chapel AME. And of all the people we might have seen and met, there stood Rep. John Lewis. Just like on that fateful day fifty years earlier, Rep. Lewis's day in 2015 started at Brown Chapel, not at the Pettus Bridge.

Brown Chapel was the training space, the experiential lab, the school where women and men who were passionate about civil rights but who were sorely unprepared for the battles, learned about nonviolent engagement with those who were equally passionate about racial segregation, discrimination, and oppression. People came to Brown Chapel to understand more fully the intimidation and abuse they would face and to ready themselves for it. At Brown Chapel, veterans of earlier marches mentored newcomers on focusing their eyesight straight ahead, as well as to how to brace themselves in the event officers and onlookers attacked them physically.

Before the marchers ever stepped foot on the Pettus Bridge, they prepared at Brown Chapel for the march. The private moments at Brown Chapel readied marchers, as much as anyone can be prepared for such a thing, for public moments at the Pettus Bridge, for the long walk along Highway 80 from Selma to Montgomery, and eventually for the chance to stand at the Alabama capitol building to demand the long-withheld right to vote for African Americans.

Friends, we need more Brown Chapels. We always have and we still do today.

A lot of things happen at a church. Worship is the church's central act. We pray and feast. We study and discuss. We enjoy fellowship and become friends of Jesus. We learn about our own commitments and the commitments of the gospel. We begin to see how much something matters to us and to what degree we are willing to act upon it. We identify ways to weigh in on issues and situations. We identify opportunities for our involvement and discern what our participation will look like.

And then comes that holy moment at the end of the worship service when from the church we are sent into the world where people and places cry out for justice and healing. That sending often gets tamped down into a sentimental blessing rather than a charge to go into the world and engage on behalf of all whose dignity has been stripped and whose community has been abandoned.

The church is a community where we prepare for the conflict that stands between the way things are now and the way God wants them to be. We are sent to be peacemakers, reconcilers, ambassadors, and doers of justice. All that calls for preparation. It calls for more congregations to think of themselves differently, to understand themselves as being more in the lineage of Brown Chapel and less only existing for the comfort of their own members.

Headed toward the conflict now,
Bill

## Questions for Discussion

1. What matters so much to you that you are willing to enter into a conflicted situation in order for people to hear your voice and know what outcome you believe is the right one for that situation?

2. What ongoing training and preparation would you like to see your congregation offer in order to better prepare to engage the issues of the day?

3. How would you like to see our nation's leaders approach conflict and how will your preferences influence how you think about and vote for candidates in the 2020 US election?

## 18

# To Support When We Can,
# to Resist When We Must

My Sisters and Brothers,

IT IS NOTHING NEW to struggle with the relationship between our faith commitments and our patriotism. From our country's beginning, people have aligned themselves at various points on a spectrum that stretches from the "freedom of religion" to the "freedom from religion."

Just think how long debates about posting the Ten Commandments in school classrooms have been going on. Or what about the practice that became prominent in the early part of the twentieth century of placing the American flag in the sanctuary? Are the cross and the flag competing symbols or complementary ones?

Wartime prayers pose a particular challenge. Do we pray for God's help and maybe even take it for granted? Do we assume God is on our side and that our enemies are automatically God's enemies? Or do we lament that humans have turned again to war and destruction that will bring suffering, in one way or another, on everyone involved? Do we convey enthusiasm or regret about war? I have heard prayers from each of those viewpoints. And what about

Jesus' radical idea of loving our enemies—do we include that in a wartime prayer?

I know many ministers who dread their congregation's worship services on the weekend nearest the Fourth of July because of the challenges posed by attempting to reconcile faith commitments and patriotism. In an attempt to keep the focus of worship on the God of all the nations, some do not include any patriotic hymns or readings in the service and do not make any mention of July 4th in their sermon. I understand that approach, but ignoring the context of that week is a missed opportunity to help people navigate the tension between faith commitments and patriotism.

Others will swing wildly in the opposite direction, over-emphasize patriotic themes, and turn the worship service into a civic celebration of our country's birthday. This probably feels really good to a lot of people, but it further clouds the relationship between our faith commitments and our patriotism when the demands and the concerns of the gospel never get raised.

And as I mentioned in a previous letter, more than a few ministers punt, take a week of vacation and come back after the cherry pie has disappeared and the supply of fireworks has been exhausted.

As is often the case, another way exists, a way that offers guidance in sorting out the complicated loyalties of God and country. If we take seriously our calling to think carefully and critically, we will join the debate with a clear mind and ask, "What does it mean to love God and what does it mean to love our country?" In doing so, we will consider afresh how statements and practices contribute to or detract from our understanding of these two loves.

For example, Alexander Campbell, one of the forebears of my church tradition, encouraged Christians in this country not to succumb to understandings or commitments that relegate God only to our national interests or constrict our concern only to ourselves. Writing in the nineteenth century, Campbell said, "Christians are of no country; they are citizens of the world; and their neighbors and fellows citizens are inhabitants of the remotest regions, whenever their distresses demand our friendly assistance."[1]

1. Watts, *Christian Faith and American Citizenship*, 52.

Jerry Falwell, on the other hand, argued and fought relent-lessly to restore the United States to what he viewed as its original principles as a Christian nation, a nation that holds a special place and destiny in God's plans. As the so-called Moral Majority was gaining traction and influence in the mid-1970s, Falwell seemed incredulous at any possible distinction between our faith commit-ments and our national loyalties, saying, "The idea that religion and politics don't mix was invented by the Devil to keep Christians from running their own country."[2]

## Why This Issue Matters

Katha Pollitt wrote that the problem of patriotism for Americans is that "it prevents us from seeing ourselves the way others see us." As a result, Americans wonder why the rest of the world doesn't love us. Patriotism keeps us from seeing that we may be regressing—class distinctions, poverty, and homelessness are increasing—and we end up living in an idealized past.[3]

We owe the leaders of our government our sincere thanks and our persistent prayer. It should be a prayer that is thankful for the willingness to serve despite the kinds of criticism and dangers with which they live. We owe our leaders and our nation ways to hold all of us accountable for abuses, injustices, the breakdown of the legislative process, and multiple systems that benefit a few while shutting others out. We also owe our leaders the courage to challenge and resist and, whenever possible, to speak construc-tively and work diligently for the sake of the character and people of this country.

There is no shortage of patriotic fervor, but there is a shortage of political resistance. It's unpatriotic to be silent when elected and appointed public figures demean individuals and exclude whole communities from the common good. Patriotism and faith both lead us to name and resist any speech or action or policy that

2. Goodman and Price, *Jerry Falwell*, 91.

3. Pollitt, "Symposium."

divides us against one another and places groups on the losing end. To live in the United States places enormous responsibility on us all. Our government only works when we give to it what is due, which is a love that actively works to make it better, even when that love gets expressed through challenge, resistance, and protest.

On the other hand, the love we owe to God is pure adoration and praise. That love is reserved for God alone. Human institutions do not function well and cannot be trusted with pure adoration and praise. I know from leading institutions and organizations how inconvenient and time-consuming it can be when questions and strong disagreements arise, but human institutions depend on loyal opposition. They need the feedback, input, and participation of a constructive, sometimes resistant love.

For those of us of European descent who participate in predominantly Caucasian congregations, we face a great challenge. We do not have much experience in resisting. We've not been toughened by doing battle with systems because we established most of those systems. It's more likely that we have been the target of resistance movements rather than participants in them. We likely have expended our energy in protecting ourselves against change and loss. We cannot delay any longer in setting things right. Too many lives are at stake and so is the character of our country.

The only way our institutions become more inclusive and fair is for those who love those institutions to celebrate their great moments and to shine the light brightly on those moments when they fall woefully short. James Baldwin said, "I love America more than any other country in the world and, exactly for this reason, I insist on the right to criticize her perpetually."[4]

## The Witness of the Church

Scripture reminds us of how long people have dealt with this challenge, even if it doesn't always clarify matters for us. Israel spent much of its biblical history being dominated by various empires

4. Baldwin, *Notes of a Native Son*, 9.

and sorting out its own questions about how they would be ruled and by whom. In the Old Testament, priests removed even the symbols of the great King David from the temple because they represented a human government and were not part of the worship of God. Even the Roman Empire decided that state symbols were inappropriate in the house of God.

Jesus' announcement that the realm of God is near is a direct challenge to the empire in which he lived and at whose hands he died. The early church understood what it was like to do battle with political power, as in this passage from Ephesians: "For our struggle is not against enemies of blood and flesh, but against the rulers, against the authorities, against the cosmic powers of this present darkness, against the spiritual forces of evil in the heavenly places."[5]

At the same time, some verses startle and disrespect the suffering of millions through time when they appear to demand uncritical loyalty, such as when Paul famously writes: "Let every person be subject to the governing authorities; for there is no authority except from God, and those authorities that exist have been instituted by God."[6] A similar urging appears in 1 Peter: "For the Lord's sake accept the authority of every human institution, whether of the emperor as supreme, or of governors, as sent by him to punish those who do wrong and to praise those who do right."[7]

As many have noted, more harm has come from obeying leaders and rulers in some instances as has come from disobeying them. The Civil Rights era in the United States included powerful acts of resistance and civil disobedience toward laws and attitudes that did not reflect the realm of God. Dr. King certainly did not assume that governing authorities were beyond accountability or criticism. For example, in his powerful speech at Riverside Church in New York entitled "Beyond Vietnam," he directly criticized our motives and involvement in Southeast Asia: "The world now demands a maturity in America that we may not be able to achieve. It demands that we admit that we have been wrong from the beginning of our adventure

5. Eph 6:12.
6. Rom 13:1.
7. 1 Pet 2:13.

in Vietnam, that we have been detrimental to the life of the Vietnamese people."[8] And yet, to illustrate the complicated relationship we have been discussing, he mentions his love for his country several times in this speech, saying, "I come to this platform tonight to make a passionate plea to my beloved nation."[9]

Now, we are living in another time when the American story and the Christian story seem to be up for grabs in this country. Fierce and fearful voices on many sides are trying to leverage both stories for political gain.

Jesus said, "Give to the emperor the things that are the emperor's, and to God the things that are God's."[10] Our task is to sort out these competing claims in the midst of an emotionally charged, often manipulative religious culture and live our lives by appropriately giving ourselves to these two loyalties, knowing and trusting always that loving God with all our heart, mind, soul, and strength remains our first commitment and the commitment that frames all others.

For an American maturity,
Bill

## Questions for Discussion

1. How do you navigate those situations where your Christian identity and your patriotic loyalty conflict with one another?

2. What policies and situations call out for resistance from the church and what form should that resistance take?

3. What will you support and what will you resist during the 2020 US campaign and election?

8. Carson and Shepherd, *Call to Conscience*, 154.
9. Carson and Shepherd, *Call to Conscience*, 141.
10. Matt 22:21.

*19*

# To Find Allies When Possible

My Sisters and Brothers,

ALLIES EXIST FOR US. And we can be allies with others. Together, we can address important causes, sometimes by building alliances among unexpected people. I begin this letter by sharing two examples of that.

First, Krista Tippett shared a Twitter exchange during an *On Being* interview that reminds us of how people are standing with each other, even as leaders work day and night to divide the country and conquer the electorate. In that exchange, Qasim Rashid, who is running for a Virginia congressional seat in 2020, says, "My faith and my duty as a neighbor command me, if any synagogue in Virginia needs help with security, I'll stand guard. An attack on a synagogue is an attack on all houses of worship." A rabbi named Michael Latz replied to him, saying, "And if your mosques need us to stand guard, I'm there, my brother. I'm there. Our love is stronger than their hate."[1] If allies can be found bridging the Muslim-Jewish divide in times of violence against both groups, the chances

---

1. Claiborne and Ghobash, "Called and Conflicted," interview, August 15, 2019.

are very good that we can find allies for the death-dealing causes that stir our hearts and call us to action.

While that first story is one of promise to stand with each other if either is ever under threat, this second story shows how people at opposite ends of the political spectrum can find creative ways to engage an issue together that will change people's lives. In doing so, all sides experienced severe criticism, but that did not stop them. It only reminded them of a dysfunctional, nasty political climate that would rather see bad situations continue than work with people across differences. That's a sorry commentary on the state of things, but it's an all-too-common scenario. "I only want to help hurting people if I can work with my people in my camp and my party." Not everybody, though, has sunk that low.

Van Jones is a political commentator and an avowed Democrat. More than that, he served in President Obama's administration as an advisor to the White House Council on Environmental Quality. So, if Jones fit into today's typical political mode, he would work generally with Democrats and, even then, probably a small subset that is particularly passionate about environmental issues, but when he came to our campus in October 2019 to speak he told a different story.

Jones began working on criminal justice reform during the Obama administration, but no legislation passed. In an unheard-of turn of events, Jones worked with the Trump administration to secure passage of the First Step Act, which reduces sentences for nonviolent offenders and supports their reentry into society. Thousands of formerly incarcerated adults have already been released as a result of this legislation. Senate Leader McConnell tried to stall this legislation and even announced that it would not be coming to the floor for a vote, but in this case an overwhelming bipartisan alliance receiving unusual support from President Trump ensured that the bill was voted on and became law.

Jones has been labeled a sellout, but not because of his support for this particular legislation. Rather, he's been called a traitor because he joined with conservatives and with President Trump to change people's lives. He acknowledges that he has many, many problems and conflicts with Trump, but the opportunity to take an important first step on criminal justice reform was at hand and it was the right thing to pursue. "There are battleground issues that we don't agree on, and we should disagree . . . That's what democracy means," Jones said. "Democracy means you don't have to agree. Dictatorship, you have to agree. My problem is not the battleground. My problem is there are common ground issues where we do agree and we won't work together on those all too often, and that has got to stop in America."[2]

## Why This Issue Matters

Allies exist for the work and the issues that matter most to us. We may share the same neighborhood with some of these allies and not know it. Impactful groups may already be addressing an issue that is important to us and we just haven't connected yet. Many of these groups have come together in common cause around situations that they believe simply cannot stand, things like gun violence, opioid addiction, generational poverty, immigration reform, public transit, and mass incarceration. These individuals and organizations look for small victories upon which they can continue to build. They usually work in circumstances that demand persistence and scrappiness in order even to begin to change laws and situations. They almost all get started with few resources, little experience, and an unclear path, but their unwavering commitment to a humane, kind, and just outcome for people who are hurting and excluded propels them into the arena of action.

The tweet between Rashid and Latz above stands out as unusual, to say the least. It's more common to follow, read, or hear about highly reactive, defensive, and bullying tweets, posts, and speeches. Those approaches draw hard lines between people and groups that discourage alliances at all and even work to undermine the collaboration and positive outcomes. People send these threatening tweets day and night and sometimes in the middle of

2. Jones, "Uncomfortable Truths, Healing Impacts."

the night. They can lead us to believe that the mood of the country is even more divided than it is, which is exactly what those tweeters want us to believe and fear. Only occasionally do encouraging, uplifting, unifying Tweets achieve any notice or capture any coverage. As a result, the good news and the corresponding potential allies go unnoticed, unappreciated, and untapped.

Writing in 1961, Thomas Merton offered insight that warrants our attention and correction now. Merton said, "In our refusal to accept the partially good intentions of others and work with them (of course prudently and with resignation to the inevitable imperfection of the result) we are unconsciously proclaiming our own malice, our own intolerance, our own lack of realism, our own ethical and political quackery. I believe the basis for valid political action can only be the recognition that the true solution to our problems is not accessible to any one isolated party or nation but that all must arrive at it by working together."[3]

Alliances matter these days because they can be reminders that people with different perspectives and affiliations can work together. Every example of that occurring is refreshing and inspiring, but that is not the only reason alliances matter. The more important reason arises because we face major challenges as individuals and communities and the country as a whole. We will not seize opportunities, solve problems, and find an equitable way forward working in isolation from each other. Any effort happening in silos will remain in silos. Progress belongs to those who can and will work across generational, racial, ethnic, political, economic, and religious differences to get things done. To paraphrase Van Jones, we cannot get lost in the differences themselves, as real as they are, when opportunities to solve problems together are right before us.

I described this work earlier as needing persistence and scrappiness. With change occurring at a fast pace and with groups trying to block and even reverse progress, sustained effort will be required. Demonstrations and rallies serve a purpose, but Dana Bainbridge, pastor at First Christian Church of San Jose, says they

3. Merton, *New Seeds*, 118.

are not enough. "I'm definitely not against demonstrations, but so often all we do is yell at each other. These days I'm less interested in demonstrations and more interested in getting people to talk to each other civilly in ways that move people towards action."[4]

## The Witness of the Church

Scripture offers a rich array of stories that turn on the helpful actions of allies. Some of them surprise us, like the story of Rahab, a prostitute in Jericho who hid two spies as the Israelites planned their attack on the city.[5]

The Gospel of Luke describes a scene in which the disciples are debating true greatness. Jesus seems to settle the argument by having a small child sit next to him, but then John keeps the conversation going by saying, "Master, we saw someone casting out demons in your name, and we tried to stop him, because he does not follow with us." But Jesus said to him, "Do not stop him; for whoever is not against you is for you."[6]

What changes when we adopt a similar spirit? Or perhaps the more pertinent question is, what does it take for us to adopt a similar spirit? Maybe turning the phrase a little reminds of what is at stake. "Do not stop those whose stated positions are different if you share the same goal. Just because they are working on a different aspect of the issue doesn't mean they are opposed to the piece of the puzzle you are working on. If people are not throwing up barriers in your way, they should not be seen as the opposition. Give thanks for all of them and stay focused! There's probably enough credit to go around if the problem is solved. And if there isn't enough credit fairly distributed, isn't the important thing still that the problem was solved? Whoever is not against you is for you."

The apostle describes the partnership we share in the gospel as originating at the Communion Table, using the Greek word

---

4. Jha, *Transforming Communities*, 30.
5. Joshua 2.
6. Luke 9:49–50.

*koinonia* in both instances. In other words, our partnership across the church does not depend on recently arriving at a common interest or outcome with a situation, but develops from our sharing the sacred meal together. We not only remember Jesus when we eat the bread and drink the wine, we re-member Jesus in the world. We are formed in that meal as Jesus' body with all our differences to be light and peace and hope and healing to the world.

In the church, we begin as partners, as allies, and move from there toward our vocation in the world. Similar partnerships are possible in the wider community when we first come together around tables to see each other as we really are, to listen in order to understand and not just to develop our argument, to begin working together, and to love the world into life again.

It's true that sometimes we cannot wait on allies to arrive and we must go forward, but some of the fruit that our efforts will bear will be in attracting allies once we get started. I cannot think of a single issue or circumstance that only affects one person. Someone else in our community is bothered by what keeps us up at night. Someone else in our community knows of the same need on which you are about to focus your energies. Someone else in the community is just waiting on you to take the first step.

Problems can be solved, but the vast majority of them cannot be solved alone. We need each other.

Willing to be your ally for good,
Bill

# Questions for Discussion

1. Does your faith cause you to believe that even the people and groups with the most radically different points of view should come together to listen to one another? Why or why not?

2. Imagine if those people or groups with radically different points of view came together, what are the real barriers to listening and learning and how would you coach them to overcome those barriers?

3. What priorities does your faith place on bridging differences and working together, and how will those priorities shape your participation in the 2020 US election?

## 20

## To Engage Constructively

My Sisters and Brothers,

LYMAN T. JOHNSON SERVED as a distinguished educator in Louisville and as an advocate for equal access and rights for African Americans. He knew the challenges firsthand as the first African American student enrolled at the University of Kentucky. Johnson used those challenges to open doors and possibilities for people who for too long had been shut out.

Johnson compared his love for his country with a leaky roof on his house. "When you say if I don't like this country then why don't I leave it, then my classic illustration is: if my house is leaking, I don't get mad at it and leave it. I just get the ladder and get me some tools and I get up on the house and I patch the leak. And that is what I'm going to do for my country—I love it; I like it. And when I see its imperfections, I'm not going to get mad at it and leave. I'm going to get mad at its imperfections."[1]

To extend Johnson's imagery and, I pray, his legacy, these letters are about gathering up our tools, getting up on the house, and fixing the leak. I hope these letters not only awaken us to critical situations in our country, but move us to engage. As I said in the

1. Hall, *Rest of the Dream*, 162.

introduction, the letters provide a starting point. They make sure some things register on your radar, but they also will prompt you to register numerous other concerns that cry out for our attention. I hope they call us out of our withdrawal and our silence. But remember, I have spent my life in the church. I know how we operate, especially those of us in privileged Eurocentric churches where the end game too often is a good discussion. Very little will change in our country if the engagement with these letters never moves beyond our personal meditation time, study groups, and church school classes.

Any response to these letters also must go beyond congregational stands and denominational resolutions. Those are not bad things, but they do not carry the influence or register the concern or initiate the desired impact on their own. Congregations sometimes adopt a stance or slogan on an issue when it's not altogether clear why this issue was chosen from the many that call out for our attention. It's also not always clear to what extent the congregation is expected to make that one stance their cause to the neglect of others about which they feel more passionate and for which their gifts and commitments seem more naturally suited.

I hope these letters offer comfort by articulating some of what we are experiencing, but I hope they create an even greater measure of discomfort. The roof is leaking and we need to do something about it. I hope these letters identify what is at stake and help you frame issues more thoughtfully to others, but in the end it does not matter how eloquently we describe the rainfall that is disrupting what we cherish and enjoy in our home. Most of all, I hope these letters move you to involvement and engagement—to gathering up your tools, getting up on the roof, and fixing the leak.

That's what an active, concrete love for our country looks like. Our discussions need to go somewhere. They need to address our glaring imperfections on our way to this "more perfect union."

## Why This Issue Matters

I find it encouraging to hear President Theodore Roosevelt's "Citizenship in a Republic" speech quoted more and more often these days. From that thirty-five page manuscript comes this memorable paragraph:

> It is not the critic who counts; not the man who points out how the strong man stumbles, or where the doer of deeds could have done them better. The credit belongs to the man who is actually in the arena, whose face is marred by dust and sweat and blood; who strives valiantly; who errs, who comes short again and again, because there is no effort without error and shortcoming; but who does actually strive to do the deeds; who knows great enthusiasms, the great devotions; who spends himself in a worthy cause; who at the best knows in the end the triumph of high achievement, and who at the worst, if he fails, at least fails while daring greatly, so that his place shall never be with those cold and timid souls who neither know victory nor defeat.[2]

Christians in this country can help to change the public conversation and the political environment by bringing a positive spirit into the arena, by articulating what matters to us, and by showing that what matters to us is greater than our fear and avoidance of conflict. To engage constructively is to move into the arena and give ourselves away in the service of a compassionate, kind, and just vision. We will not all enter the same arena. Each of us will pick a particular opportunity or issue that calls to us. None of us can do it all, but we can all do something. We will need to focus tightly on that opportunity or issue. Get very specific about it. Vagueness about what we want to change diminishes our chances of changing anything and further entrenches the status quo. Articulate the urgency about your issue so that others will feel that urgency, too.

Perhaps your cause is to disrupt generational poverty, or to work on humane immigration polices and practices, or to address

2. Roosevelt, "Citizenship in a Republic."

gun violence and sensible gun access and ownership, or to come alongside the mentally ill and physically disabled, or to lobby for healthcare that benefits all Americans, or to restore the rights of felons for a fulfilling and productive reentry to society. A hundred arenas exist where our gifts and energy will make a difference. They are all part of a large arena where we pursue the highest, best quality of life possible for everyone. The cause to which we feel called may not be listed above, but you know what it is and you can be the champion for that cause through your advocacy and direct action.

"Constructively" is a key word here. We can point to a lot of engagement, but so much of it is destructive, splintering, self-serving, and dreadfully shortsighted. Rarely do we hear people working together from the presumption of good faith and arriving at a compromise that, at least for the immediate future, serves the American people well. Instead, a bitter divide leads people to make unreasonable and one-sided demands, attack people on the opposing side, and undermine what might otherwise be constructive efforts.

And remember, others are in the arena advocating for their positions. The Moral Majority may get credited with electing Ronald Reagan, but they were just as effective at the local level recruiting precinct captains, reshaping school boards, placing local referenda on ballots, and working for passage of state statutes that represented their values. The Moral Majority ran its course as an organization, but voices like it are still in the arena. Our best hope is to be in the arena with them, shaping the conversation and the legislation to benefit a wider segment of our population. And if being in the arena with them means we come to see each other in a new way, build unexpected relationships, and find a constructive, common path forward, God be praised! Instead of winning arguments, let's create some victories for people.

## The Witness of the Church

In this section in the preceding letters, I have drawn on Scripture and Christian tradition to speak about the witness of the church.

This letter, though, calls for something else. It reads more like a roll call of the saints who have engaged constructively in times of opportunity and challenge and who, through their example, call and inspire us to do the same.

Let's begin with Doris. She was nearly sixty years old when she became aware of the number of adults in her home county who either could not read at all or who read at a very low level. Doris saw how economically and emotionally crippling this was to so many kind and decent people, so she began an adult learning center. She recruited volunteers, raised money from a variety of sources, advertised the services, and began helping adults to learn to read. Doris was not a trained educator or a professional fundraiser or marketing strategist. She saw a need and, at a time when retirement should have been on the horizon, engaged constructively.

Dorothy and her family lived on the same farm that three previous generations had worked, but family farms were not faring well at the time and, of course, that situation has not improved. It made economic sense for Dorothy to sell their house and land and move to town, but like so many across the South and Midwest, her life and identity could not be understood apart from her farm. So she helped to organize a statewide alliance that gave family farmers a place to find support, understand options, secure resources, and lobby state legislators. Later, she would represent the national organization of community farm alliances at a US congressional hearing that led to some supportive legislative measures. Dorothy wasn't a community organizer or a public voice or a political insider. She saw a need and, at a time when she could have cashed out and moved on, engaged constructively.

Alejandro and Martina experienced homelessness for several weeks after Hurricane Katrina. The restaurant where they worked as chefs was completely destroyed, as was the apartment building where they had lived for seven years. They moved to Cincinnati and started over—a new home, a new community, and new jobs—but they never forgot the experience of being homeless. Martina heard that area churches were forming a local chapter of the Interfaith Hospitality Network, an organization that coordinates housing for homeless families by utilizing space and volunteers of congregations. They approached their church about becoming a sponsoring congregation, even though they had only been attending there a few months. They spent hours with the families, sharing their own story and offering comfort and encouragement to people who needed it the most. Alejandro and Martina aren't social workers or chaplains or facility managers. They saw a need, one that they knew a lot about, and they engaged constructively.

I can tell you a hundred stories like these, but since you are reading this book you may already be in the arena that Theodore Roosevelt talked about. You may be someone who is already engaging constructively, somebody who saw a need that should not stand and despite a lack of qualifications and experience, went to work to address it. If that's you, I give thanks. And I give thanks for everyone else who is about to engage constructively for the good of us all.

In the arena with you,
Bill

## Questions for Discussion

1. What will help you to become involved in policies and situations that you care deeply about and that will impact people you love and value?

2. In what area do you wish to be prepared and equipped in order to have a positive impact in your community and where will you find the needed resources to prepare and equip you?

3. What will your church and our country look like four years from now if you remain silent and do not engage issues and situations that cry out for healing and justice during the 2020 US campaign and election?

# Now That the Election Is Over

My Sisters and Brothers,

I AM WRITING TO you in late February and it is a humbling and sobering experience to do so. I am writing about the aftermath of an election—a critical election—that is not going to take place for eight more months. It reminds me of times in the past when I wrote Christmas Eve sermons for a preaching journal. Because of the editing process and the publishing schedule, I needed to write and submit my Christmas Eve sermon months in advance. Even though Christmas speaks to my faith in deep ways with its themes of hope, incarnation and light, it still took considerable effort to put myself in the Christmas spirit in the middle of summer.

Still, it seems needed and appropriate to conclude this collection with such a letter for those days in November when we are gathering ourselves following the election and preparing for what comes next. The season for primaries and conventions has come and gone and we have lived through a general election campaign that has been brutal in nature and incredibly myopic in focus. The race for president came down to a handful of states. We know now who will be the president of the United States for the next four years. Now that the election is over, what lies ahead for you, for me, and for our country? What will continue and what must change? And again, what will the witness of the church be?

Even this far in advance, I think I can paint a fairly accurate picture of how things will be following November 3, 2020. I bet you can as well. Whatever the outcome of the election, we will continue to struggle to some degree as a country with the issues and spirit that characterize the Era of Trump.

If President Trump is defeated, some of us will feel a surge of hopeful energy. A vision recently articulated by President Jimmy Carter will lift our spirits and our sights toward a new day where "a strong nation, like a strong person, can afford to be gentle, firm, thoughtful, and restrained. It can afford to extend a helping hand to others. It is a weak nation, like a weak person, that must behave with bluster and boasting and rashness and other signs of insecurity."[1] We will believe again that we can come together as a country to overcome a brutal election season, address challenges with values and polices that honor the dignity of every person and deal honestly with the complexity of the issues at hand.

If the president is defeated in his bid for reelection, we will trust again that the better angels of our nature will revive the mystic chords of our memory and swell again our affection, as President Lincoln said at his first inaugural,[2] but we still will be facing enormous challenges with little consensual political capital upon which to draw. As I said in the introduction to this collection, the era of Trump will not end when his presidency does. While a Trump presidency highlights and exacerbates certain issues and aided his election in the first place, those issues are too large and entangled to simply go away on his last day in the White House.

If the president is reelected, we will get more of what we have known the last four years—coarse rhetoric, unrestrained bombast, interference in situations beyond his purview and perhaps beyond the law, and a continued reshaping of American values. This will delight some people. In fact, some people will have voted for him for exactly these reasons. If the president is reelected, his erratic approach and divisive demeanor will increase the feeling of always being on edge and off balance. He feels little restraint now, even to the point of badgering lawyers and bullying judges in already settled legal cases. If the country gives him a second four-year term,

1. Carter, *Presidential Campaign*, 1008.
2. Lincoln, *Great Speeches*, 61.

he will take the country into even deeper extremes and gridlock. Again, it appears now that is what about half the country wants to see. That half supports the president for these very reasons. Those who make up that half of the country believe the country needs to be shaken up even more and that President Trump is the one for the job.

The division will continue, so will the lack of political will and imagination. That means that economic disparity, a crisis in healthcare, shameful and inhumane behavior at the US-Mexico border, and gun violence will continue, too. It means that more fringe groups like white nationalists will work their way into the mainstream. It means that the escalation of money's influence will continue, that the judicial system will have lost a little more of its independence, and that individuals and communities who have been locked out of systems for too long already will slip further into despair and destitution.

So far in 2020, the Senate acquitted the president after the House impeached him. He used the State of the Union address as a campaign rally. He chose not to shake Speaker Pelosi's hand and she tore up his speech in a public demonstration of disgust. Neither of those actions rise to the vision of our better angels.

In what many viewed as a stunning act, the president awarded Rush Limbaugh the Presidential Medal Freedom. Limbaugh is not the first questionable recipient of that distinguished award, but like in most things, you get more of what you reward. I would rather see more Elie Wiesel and Maya Angelou types.

You will have witnessed the Democratic nominating process unfold with their debates, primaries, and convention. You, no doubt, have your own thoughts on whether the Democrats nominated the right person to oppose the president. You know whether they eventually worked through the early tension between revolutionary change and incremental change. Depending on the outcome, your preferred candidate and how the campaign season unfolded, you may be asking a lot of "what if" questions about now. In this last letter, I am asking a different question.

## What Time Is It?

I suppose writing a letter in February to talk about an unknown outcome in November might cause us to ask, "What time is it?"

For some, this is a wonderful time. They support the president and they like the direction in which the country is going. They believe America is either great again or at least on its way toward that goal. For others, it feels like what they value and appreciate most about our country is under siege. That group wonders if it is too late to recover what makes America great.

I have heard people put it in more apocalyptic terms. They say, "We are not in complete meltdown and we are not at a point of no return, but I worry that a major crisis could put our country there in ways that would involve a very long recovery." Even Rev. Jha contends that already we should be thinking in terms of a fifty-year process in creating a country for all people.[3] If that is true, many of us will not see the outcome. As a result, the life that we want for the generations that follow us will motivate whatever contributions we make toward our country's quality of life. That's always what elections are about. It just seems even truer and more urgent with this one.

For all our missteps and sins, I believe our country's story is worth sustaining. Our environment is worth protecting. The positive impact we can have in the world is worth our work toward recovering our national strength and working well with our international neighbors. Even though we may not agree on what time it is and we definitely do not express our love of country in the same ways, I believe a good many people from the left, the right, and the center want to resist the idea that it is too late to be an honorable, beneficent, and sustainable country.

Before the primaries began, Pete Buttigieg asked what I believe to be the critical question. "What do we want more than winning?" However we identify—whether it's as Republican or Democrat, conservative or progressive, or the many other ways we describe ourselves—what do we want more than the victory, the

---

3. Jha, *Transforming Communities*, 5.

office, the position or the status? What do we want more than just to say, "I beat you?" Whatever that is, it's time to move toward that. That's what time it is. We have demonstrated over and over how our winning has not led to other people winning. It's time to want something more than that, something that pulls us into a future where all are included, valued, and contributing.

## The Witness of the Church

Time is important to Christians. Scripture tells that "for everything there is a season, and a time for every matter under heaven."[4] In the Acts of the Apostles, just before Jesus' ascension, the apostles asked, "Is this the time when you will restore the Realm [Kingdom] to Israel?"[5] The psalmist asks, "How long, O Lord? Will you forget me forever? How long will you hide your face from me? How long must I bear pain in my soul?"[6]

In other places, Scripture features various people and groups attempting to predict the timing of future events, including the return of Jesus. We build our worship around seasons and holy days so that we can understand and embody more deeply the life of Jesus in the world. Time matters to us personally as we journey through seasons of joy and loss, all the while trusting that God journeys with us in every season, even if we sometimes can only see God's presence in retrospect.

The New Testament talks of *chronos*, from which we get the word chronology. *Chronos* is the marking of time, the passing of days and years. We can open our calendars and understand *chronos*.

*Kairos*, on the other hand, is the rich confluence of the life-giving spirit of God, a ripe set of circumstances and our courageous participation in the new and hopeful thing that is emerging. We open our hearts to recognize and share in *kairos*.

---

4. Eccl 3:1.
5. Acts 1:6.
6. Ps 13:1–2a.

I am hoping for the witness of the church to point toward a *kairos* season, a time when the inbreaking of God's purposes finds a ripe and receptive audience. I hope we can reclaim love as the more excellent way, a way that we look to first and always as a way forward together. I hope it is a time when our nation commits afresh to thoughtful dialogue, compassionate collaboration, and mutually beneficial outcomes.

I hope it is a time when we examine our political alignment and rise above any complicity for which we are culpable from our associations with elected leaders, campaign strategists, candidates, and lobbyists. I hope we confess when we are more part of the problem than the solution and make a course correction right away.

I hope we will sing again the great Woody Guthrie song, affirming that this land is *your* land *and* this land is *my* land and recognizing that anything short of that shared stewardship dooms us all. I hope that we can, as John Lewis said of Dr. King, produce light in dark places for the sake of trust, community, and equality.[7]

I hope we will grieve well our losses so that we can embrace and be embraced by the new life to which God calls us. I hope we will resist the narrow, fearful constraints that some would place on us in order to inhabit a larger life, one in which we consistently show up as our best selves, full of courage and vision.

I hope, in the prayer of 1 Kings, that God will give to all who serve "an understanding mind to govern your people, able to discern between good and evil."[8] Moreover, when those who govern cannot and will not make this distinction and abide by it, I hope the church will call them out and demand that goodwill and good acts characterize the decisions that those who govern must make.

I hope we in the church will conduct our own discernment and resolution of challenging issues in a way that sets an example for others to follow. I hope our approach becomes the model for a polarized country to adopt. In the midst of hateful speech and despicable posturing, may our spirit and transparency infuse all our country's conversations with a breath of fresh air.

7. Lewis, as quoted in Carson and Shepherd, *Call to Conscience*, 112.

8. 1 Kgs 3:9.

Regardless of the time of the year, my hope is something close to a Christmas hope. I hope that heaven and earth will come together in a baby and that we are open to the way that child will reveal the heart of God to us. I hope our attention to the way Jesus lives among us and interacts with us becomes the model for how we live and interact with each other.

I hope for a *kairos* church, one in which the presence and purposes of God shape our life together. I hope for a *kairos* church that will model for the world around us a way to bring diverse people together in conversation. I hope for a *kairos* church, one that God sends into the world to bless, heal, and make right.

Whatever has happened on November 3, I know from where my help and comfort come and I hope you will agree with me on what time it is. It is time for us to worship with glad hearts, to enrich our lives with deep study, to abide with sisters and brothers in the fellowship of Christ, and to serve this world that God loves so much.

See you in church,
Bill

## Questions for Discussion

1. What do you celebrate and what do you regret about the 2020 US election and your part in it?

2. Now that the 2020 US election is over, what kind of future do you hope our elected leaders work for in the United States?

3. How will your faith continue to inform and shape your participation in the church and the broader community?

# Bibliography

Alexander, Michelle. "Injustice on Repeat." *New York Times*, January 19, 2020.

Baldwin, James. *Notes of a Native Son*. Boston: Beacon, 2012.

Behrmann, Savannah. "Nikki Haley: Confederate Flag was 'Hijacked' after Charleston Church Shooting." *USA Today*, December 6, 2019. https://www.usatoday.com/story/news/politics/2019/12/06/nikki-haley-confederate-flag-hijacked-after-charleston-church-shooting/4358890002/

Brown, Brené. *Braving the Wilderness*. New York: Random House, 2016.

Campbell, Alexander, and Robert Owen. *Evidences of Christianity*. Cincinnati: Morgan, 1852.

Carson, Clayborne, and Kris Shepherd, eds. *A Call to Conscience: The Landmark Speeches of Dr. Martin Luther King, Jr.* New York: Grand Central, 2002.

Carter, Jimmy. *The Presidential Campaign, 1976*. Washington: United States Government Printing Office, 1978.

Church of the Brethren. "Church of the Brethren Statements on Slavery." July 2008. http://www.brethren.org/peacebuilding/moderndayslavery.html.

Claiborne, Shane, and Omar Saif Ghobash. "Called and Conflicted." Interview with Krista Tippett. *On Being*, August 15, 2019. https://onbeing.org/programs/shane-claiborne-and-omar-saif-ghobash-called-and-conflicted/.

Cone, James H. *Black Theology and Black Power*. Maryknoll: Orbis, 2018.

Douthat, Ross. "The Stories That Divide Us." *New York Times*, July 28, 2019.

Episcopal Church. *Enriching Our Worship 1*. New York: Church, 2000.

Frey, William H. "The U.S. Will Become 'Minority White' in 2045: Youthful Minorities Are the Engine of Future Growth." Brookings.edu. March 14, 2018. https://www.brookings.edu/blog/the-avenue/2018/03/14/the-us-will-become-minority-white-in-2045-census-projects/.

Gillette, Carolyn Winfrey. "If We Just Talk of Thoughts and Prayers." Hymn. https://www.carolynshymns.com/if_we_just_talk_of_thoughts_and_prayers.html.

Goodman, William R., and James J. H. Price. *Jerry Falwell: An Unauthorized Profile*. Lynchburg, VA: Paris, 1981.

# Bibliography

Hall, Wade. *The Rest of the Dream: The Black Odyssey of Lyman Johnson.* Lexington: University Press of Kentucky, 1988.

Heifetz, Ronald. *Leadership without Easy Answers.* Cambridge: Harvard University Press, 1994.

Hilton, Allen. *A House United: How the Church Can Save the World.* Minneapolis: Fortress, 2018.

Hing, Bill Ong. *American Presidents, Deportations and Human Rights Violations.* London: Cambridge University Press, 2018.

Hockenos, Matthew D. *Then They Came for Me: Martin Niemoller, the Pastor Who Defied the Nazies.* New York: Basic Books, 2018.

Jha, Sandhya Rani. *Transforming Communities: How People Like You Are Healing Their Neighborhoods.* St. Louis: Chalice, 2017.

Jones, Van. "Uncomfortable Truths, Healing Impacts." Presentation given at Christian Theological Seminary, Indianapolis, Indiana, October 1, 2019.

Kahneman, Daniel. *Thinking Fast and Slow.* New York: Farrar, Straus and Giroux, 2013.

Kaur, Harmeet. "A New Jersey Religious College Will Set Aside Nearly $28 Million for Slavery Reparations." CNN.com, October 26, 2019. https://www.cnn.com/2019/10/26/us/princeton-seminary-slavery-reparations-trnd/index.html.

King, Martin Luther, Jr. *Why We Can't Wait.* Boston: Beacon, 2011.

Kipling, Rudyard. "If." In *Kipling: Poems.* New York: Everyman's Library, 2007.

Kurzweil, Ray. "Breakfast with the Financial." Interview with Caroline Daniel. *Financial Times,* April 10, 2015. Interview at https://www.ft.com/content/9ed80e14-dd11-11e4-a772-0144feab7de.

Lincoln, Abraham. *Great Speeches.* Mineola, NY: Dover, 1991.

Liptack, Adam. "Chief Justice Defends Judicial Independence." *New York Times,* November 21, 2018. https://www.nytimes.com/2018/11/21/us/politics/trump-chief-justice-roberts-rebuke.html.

Merton, Thomas. *New Seeds of Contemplation.* New York: New Directions, 1961.

Morin, Rebecca. "Immigration Official Ken Cuccinelli: Statue of Liberty Poem Refers to Immigrants from Europe." *USA Today,* August 13, 2019. https://www.usatoday.com/story/news/politics/2019/08/13/ken-cuccinelli-statue-liberty-poem-refers-migrants-europe/2004455001/.

Paulsen, David. "$1.7 Million for Slavery Reparations Fund Puts Virginia Theological Seminary at Forefront of Debate." Episcopal News Service. September 6, 2019. https://www.episcopalnewsservice.org/2019/09/06/1-7-million-for-slavery-reparations-fund-puts-virginia-theological-seminary-at-forefront-of-debate/.

Peterson, Eugene. *Pastor: A Memoir.* New York: HarperOne, 2011.

Pollitt, Katha. "Symposium: Katha Pollitt." *Dissent,* Winter 2010.

Ramsey, G. Lee, Jr. *Care-full Preaching: From Sermon to Caring Community.* Eugene, OR: Wipf and Stock, 2012.

# Bibliography

Roosevelt, Theodore. "Citizenship in a Republic." Speech given in Paris, France, April 23, 1910.

Schade, Leah. *Preaching in the Purple Zone: Ministry in the Red-Blue Divide.* Lanham, MD: Rowman & Littlefield, 2019.

Scott, Susan. *Fierce Conversations: Achieving Success at Work and in Life One Conversation at a Time.* New York: Berkley, 2004.

Smith, Christopher C. *How the Body of Christ Talks.* Grand Rapids: Brazos, 2019.

Southern Baptist Convention. "Resolution on Racial Reconciliation on the 150th Anniversary of the Southern Baptist Convention." Atlanta. 1995. http://www.sbc.net/resolutions/899/resolution-on-racial-reconciliation-on-the-150th-anniversary-of-the-southern-baptist-convention.

Trump, Donald. *The Art of the Deal.* New York: Random House, 1987.

———. "We're Going to Win So Much." Video from campaign rally, Albany, NY, 2016. https://www.cnn.com/videos/politics/2017/08/18/trump-albany-rally-winning-sot.cnn.

Tutu, Desmond. *God Has a Dream.* New York: Doubleday, 2004.

United States Census Bureau. 1960 Census of the Population. https://www.census.gov/library/publications/1961/dec/pc-s1-10.html.

Yeats, W. B. "The Second Coming." In *The Collected Poems of W. B. Yeats.* New York: Collier, 1989. Poem available at https://www.poetryfoundation.org/poems/43290/the-second-coming.

Made in the USA
Monee, IL
30 July 2020